John Philip Newman

The triple Key to unlock the Kingdom of Heaven

The Way, the Truth, the Life

John Philip Newman

The triple Key to unlock the Kingdom of Heaven
The Way, the Truth, the Life

ISBN/EAN: 9783337148362

Printed in Europe, USA, Canada, Australia, Japan

Cover: Foto ©Lupo / pixelio.de

More available books at **www.hansebooks.com**

THE TRIPLE KEY

TO UNLOCK

THE KINGDOM OF HEAVEN

THE WAY, THE TRUTH, THE LIFE

And I saw an . . . ANGEL come down from heaven . . . and he had in his hand a LITTLE BOOK open

NEW YORK
PRINTED BY HUNT & EATON
150 FIFTH AVENUE
1891

TO

ALL WHO HAVE LEARNED THE

PASS-WORD

THAT TURNS THE TRIPLE KEY IN ITS

COMBINATION LOCK,

AND

WILL TEACH THE SAME

THE WORDS OF THIS LITTLE BOOK ARE

𝔗𝔫𝔰𝔠𝔯𝔦𝔟𝔢𝔡.

Pray for my soul. More things are wrought
    by prayer
Than the world dreams of. Wherefore, let thy
    voice
Rise like a fountain for me night and day.
For what are men better than sheep or goats,
That nourish a blind LIFE within the brain,
If, knowing God, they lift not hands of prayer
Both for themselves and those who call them
    friend?
For so the whole round earth in every WAY
Bound by gold chains about the feet of God.
—Tennyson.

PROLUSION.

DEFINITION OF

By NOAH WEBSTER, LL.D.

ONE. A moving; passage; progression; transit; journey.

I prythee, now, lead the WAY.—SHAK.

2. That by which one passes or progresses; opportunity or room to pass; place of passing; passage; road or path of any kind.

To find the WAY to heaven.—SHAK.

Perhaps the WAY seems difficult.—MILTON.

The season and WAYS were very improper for his majesty's forces to march so great a distance.—EVELYN.

3. Length of space; distance; interval; as, a great WAY; a long WAY.

4. Course, or direction of motion or progress; tendency of action; advance.

If that WAY be your walk, you have not far.—MILTON.

And let eternal justice take the WAY.—DRYDEN.

5. Means by which any thing is reached, or any thing is accomplished; scheme; device.

My best WAY is to creep under.—SHAK.

By noble WAYS we conquests will prepare.—DRYDEN.

What impious WAYS my wishes took!—PRIOR.

6. Manner; method; mode; fashion; as, the WAY of expressing one's ideas.

7. Regular course; habitual method of life or action; plan of conduct; mode of dealing.

Having lost the WAY of nobleness.—SIDNEY.

All flesh had corrupted his WAY upon the earth.—GEN. 6. 12.

Her WAYS are WAYS of pleasantness, and all her paths are peace.—PROV. 3. 17.

8. Determined course; resolved mode of action or conduct; as, to have one's WAY.

9. Progress; as, a ship has WAY; the timbers on which a ship is launched.

10. By the WAY; by the WAY of; covert WAY; half-WAY; milky WAY. "We are quite out of the WAY."—LOCKE. Right of WAY (law). HighWAY.

WAY.

L O, I come (in the volume of the Book it is written of me) to do thy will, O God.
—Heb. 10. 7.

This is his NAME whereby he shall be called, THE LORD OUR RIGHTEOUS-NESS. —Prophet Jer. 23. 6.

Thou shalt call his NAME JESUS: for he shall save his people from their sins. . . . EMMANUEL, God with us. —Matt. 1. 21, 23.

Neither is there salvation in any other: for there is none other NAME under heaven given among men, whereby we must be saved.
—Acts 4. 12.

Wherefore God also hath highly exalted him, and given him a NAME which is above every NAME: that at the NAME of JESUS every knee should bow, of things in heaven, and things in earth, and things under the earth; and that every tongue should confess that Jesus Christ is Lord, to the glory of God the Father. —Phil. 2. 9-11.

Far above all principality, and power, and might, and dominion, and every NAME that is named, not only in this world, but also in that which is to come: and hath put all things under his feet, and gave him to be the head over all things to the church, which is his body, the fullness of him that filleth all in all.
—Eph. 1. 21-23.

In whom ye also trusted, after that ye heard the word of TRUTH, the gospel of your salvation: in whom also, after that ye believed, ye were sealed with that Holy Spirit of promise, which is the earnest of our inheritance until the redemption of the purchased possession, unto the praise of his glory.
—Eph. 1. 13, 14.

And in his NAME shall the Gentiles trust.
—Matt. 12. 21.

But to us there is but one God, the Father, of whom are all things, and we in him; and one Lord Jesus Christ, by whom are all things, and we by him. —1 Cor. 8. 6.

One God and Father of all, who is above all, and through all, and in you all. —Eph. 4. 6.

Jesus saith, I am the WAY, the TRUTH, and the LIFE. —John 14. 6.

And have ye not read this Scripture; The stone which the builders rejected is become the head of the corner?
—Mark 12. 10.

And [Jesus] began to say unto them [disciples], This day is this Scripture fulfilled in your ears.
—Luke 4. 21.

And they believed the Scripture, and the word which Jesus had said. —John 2. 22.

I will give unto thee the keys of the kingdom of heaven.—Matt. 16. 19.

This lamp through all the tedious night
  Of LIFE shall guide my WAY;
Till we behold the clearer light
  Of an eternal day. —John Fawcett.

Lead, kindly Light, amid the encircling gloom,
  Lead thou me on!
The night is dark, and I am far from home;
  Lead thou me on!
Keep thou my feet; I do not ask to see
The distant scene; one step enough for me.
  —John H. Newman.

And follow, safely trusting him who guides;
  Who never path of wrong or folly trod—
In whose tried LIFE no least dishonor hides,
  To him is given to know the WAYS of God.
  —M. L. Dickinson.

Old Testament.

He placed at the east of the garden of Eden cherubim, and a flaming sword which turned every WAY, to keep the WAY of the tree of LIFE. —Gen. 3. 24.

And the angel of the Lord found her by a fountain of water in the wilderness, by the fountain in the WAY to Shur. —Gen. 16. 7.

And Abraham went with them to bring them on the WAY. —Gen. 18. 16.

For I know him, that he will command his children and his household after him, and they shall keep the WAY of the Lord, to do justice and judgment. —Gen. 18. 19.

I being in the WAY, the Lord led me.
—Gen. 24. 27.

And he said unto me, The Lord, before whom I walk, will send his angel with thee, and prosper thy WAY ; and thou shalt take a wife for my son of my kindred, and of my father's house. —Gen. 24. 40.

And said, O Lord God of my master Abraham, if now thou do prosper my WAY which I go. —Gen. 24. 42.

Hinder me not, seeing the Lord hath prospered my WAY. —Gen. 24. 56.

And the servant took Rebekah, and went his WAY. —Gen. 24. 61.

And Jacob vowed a vow, saying, If God will be with me, and will keep me in this WAY that I go, and will give me bread to eat and raiment to put on, so that I come again to my father's house in peace; then shall the Lord be my God. —Gen. 28. 20, 21.

And Jacob went on his WAY, and the angels of God met him. And when Jacob saw them, he said, This is God's host.
—Gen. 32. 1, 2.

And let us arise, and go up to Beth-el; and I will make there an altar unto God, who answered me in the day of my distress, and was with me in the WAY which I went.—Gen. 35. 3.

Joseph commanded to . . . give them provision for the WAY. —Gen. 42. 25.

Be thou for the people to Godward, that thou mayest bring the causes unto God: and thou shalt teach them ordinances and laws, and shalt show them the WAY wherein they must walk, and the work that they must do.
—Exod. 18. 19, 20.

And Moses let his father-in-law depart; and he went his WAY into his own land.
—Exod. 18. 27.

Behold, I send an Angel before thee, to keep thee in the WAY, and to bring thee into the place which I have prepared. —Exod. 23. 20.

I pray thee, if I have found grace in thy sight, show me now thy WAY, that I may know thee, that I may find grace in thy sight: and consider that this nation is thy people.
—Exod. 33. 13.

We will go by the king's high WAY, we will not turn to the right hand nor to the left.
—Num. 20. 17.

Then the Lord opened the eyes of Balaam, and he saw the angel of the Lord standing in the WAY. —Num. 22. 31.

Thou shalt teach them diligently unto thy

children, and shalt talk of them when thou sittest in thine house, and when thou walkest by the WAY, and when thou liest down, and when thou risest up. —Deut. 6. 7.

Thou shalt remember all the WAY which the Lord thy God led thee. —Deut. 8. 2.

To love the Lord your God, to walk in all his WAYS, and to cleave unto him. —Deut. 11. 22.

Thou hast avouched the Lord this day to be thy God, and to walk in his WAYS, and to keep his statutes, and his commandments.
—Deut. 26. 17.

The Lord shall establish thee a holy people unto himself, as he hath sworn unto thee, if thou shalt keep the commandments of the Lord thy God, and walk in his WAYS. And all people of the earth shall see that thou art called by the name of the Lord; and they shall be afraid of thee. —Deut. 28. 9, 10.

This book of the law shall not depart out of thy mouth; but thou shalt meditate therein day and night, that thou mayest observe to do according to all that is written therein: for

then thou shalt make thy WAY prosperous, and then thou shalt have good success.
—Josh. 1. 8.

Come not near unto it, that ye may know the WAY by which ye must go: for ye have not passed this WAY heretofore. —Josh. 3. 4.

For the Lord our God, he it is that brought us up and our fathers out of the land of Egypt, from the house of bondage, and which did those great signs in our sight, and preserved us in all the WAY wherein we went, and among all the people through whom we passed.
—Josh. 24. 17.

Ask counsel, we pray thee, of God, that we may know whether our WAY which we go shall be prosperous. And the priest said unto them, Go in peace: before the Lord is your WAY wherein ye go. —Judg. 18. 5, 6.

Wherefore she went forth out of the place where she was, and her two daughters-in-law with her; and they went on the WAY to return unto the land of Judah. And Naomi said, . . . Go, return each to her mother's

house: the Lord deal kindly with you. . . . The Lord grant you that ye may find rest.
—Ruth 1. 7, 8, 9.

And she said, Let thine handmaid find grace in thy sight. So the woman [Hannah] went her WAY, and did eat, and her countenance was no more sad. —1 Sam. 1. 18.

And see, if it [the ark] goeth up by the WAY of his own coast. . . . And the kine took the straight WAY to the WAY of Beth-she-mesh, and went along the highWAY, lowing as they went, and turned not aside to the right hand or to the left. —1 Sam. 6. 9, 12.

And he said unto him, Behold now, there is in this city a man of God, and he is an honorable man; all that he saith cometh surely to pass: now let us go thither; peradventure he can show us our WAY that we should go.
—1 Sam. 9. 6.

Moreover as for me, God forbid that I should sin against the Lord in ceasing to pray for you: but I will teach you the good and the right WAY. —1 Sam. 12. 23.

And David behaved himself wisely in all his WAYS; and the Lord was with him.
—1 Sam. 18. 14.

Then Saul said to David, Blessed be thou, my son David: thou shalt both do great things, and also shalt still prevail. So David went on his WAY. —1 Sam. 26. 25.

I pray thee, hearken thou also unto the voice of thine handmaid, and let me set a morsel of bread before thee; and eat, that thou mayest have strength, when thou goest on thy WAY.
—1 Sam. 28. 22.

Thy servant will go a little WAY over Jordan with the king: and why should the king recompense it me with such a reward?
—2 Sam. 19. 36.

I have kept the WAYS of the Lord, and have not wickedly departed from my God.
—2 Sam. 22. 22.

As for God, his WAY is perfect; the word of the Lord is tried: he is a buckler to all them that trust in him. —2 Sam. 22. 31.

God is my strength and power; and he maketh my WAY perfect. —2 Sam. 22. 33.

Hear thou in heaven, and forgive the sin of thy servants, and of thy people Israel, that thou teach them the good WAY wherein they should walk. —1 Kings 8. 36.

Hear thou in heaven thy dwelling-place, and forgive, and do, and give to every man according to his WAYS, whose heart thou knowest; (for thou, even thou only, knowest the hearts of all the children of men.) —1 Kings 8. 39.

That he may incline our hearts unto him, to walk in all his WAYS, and to keep his commandments, and his statutes, and his judgments, which he commanded our fathers.
—1 Kings 8. 58.

And the Lord said unto him, Go, return on thy WAY to the wilderness of Damascus: and when thou comest, anoint Hazael to be king over Syria. —1 Kings 19. 15.

He walked in all the WAYS of Asa his father; he turned not aside from it, doing that which was right in the eyes of the Lord.
—1 Kings 22. 43.

And he [Josiah] did that which was right in

the sight of the Lord, and walked in all the WAY of David his father, and turned not aside to the right hand or to the left. —2 Kings 22. 2.

When thou hast taught them the good WAY, wherein they should walk.
—2 Chron. 6. 27.

So Jotham became mighty, because he prepared his WAYS before the Lord his God.
—2 Chron. 27. 6.

To seek of him a right WAY for us, and for our little ones, and for all our substance.
—Ezra 8. 21.

Then he said, Go your WAY, ... and send portions unto them for whom nothing is prepared: for this day is holy unto our Lord: neither be ye sorry; for the joy of the Lord is your strength. ... And all the people went their WAY to eat, and to drink, and to send portions. —Neh. 8. 10-12.

The pillar of the cloud departed not from them by day, to lead them in the WAY; neither the pillar of fire by night, to show them light, and the WAY wherein they should go.
—Neh. 9. 19.

Then Esther bade them return Mordecai this answer, Go, gather together all the Jews that are present in Shushan, and fast ye for me, and neither eat nor drink three days, night or day: I also and my maidens will fast likewise; and so will I go in unto the king, which is not according to the law: and if I perish, I perish. So Mordecai went his WAY, and did according to all that Esther had commanded him.
—Esth. 4. 15-17.

Is not this thy fear, thy confidence, thy hope, and the uprightness of thy WAYS?
—Job 4. 6.

He knoweth the WAY that I take: when he hath tried me, I shall come forth as gold.
—Job 23. 10.

My foot hath held his steps, his WAY have I kept, and not declined. —Job 23. 11.

But Job answered and said, . . . Lo, these are parts of his WAYS; but how little a portion is heard of him? but the thunder of his power who can understand. —Job 26. 1, 14.

I chose out their WAY, and sat chief, and dwelt as a king in the army, as one that comforteth the mourners. —Job 29. 25.

Doth he not see my WAYS, and count all my steps? —Job 31. 4.

Blessed is the man that walketh not in the counsel of the ungodly, nor standeth in the WAY of sinners, nor sitteth in the seat of the scornful. —Psa. 1. 1.

Kiss the Son, lest he be angry, and ye perish from the WAY, when his wrath is kindled but a little. —Psa. 2. 12.

Lead me, O Lord, in thy righteousness; . . . make thy WAY straight before my face.
—Psa. 5. 8.

It is God that girdeth me with strength, and maketh my WAY perfect. —Psa. 18. 32.

Show me thy WAYS, O Lord; teach me thy paths. —Psa. 25. 4.

Good and upright is the Lord: therefore will he teach sinners in the WAY. —Psa. 25. 8.

The meek will he guide in judgment: and the meek will he teach his WAY. —Psa. 25. 9.

Teach me thy WAY, O Lord, and lead me in a plain path, because of mine enemies.
—Psa. 27. 11.

I will instruct thee and teach thee in the WAY which thou shalt go: I will guide thee with mine eye. —Psa. 32. 8.

Wait on the Lord, and keep his WAY, and he shall exalt thee to inherit the land.
—Psa. 37. 34.

I said, I will take heed to my WAYS, that I sin not with my tongue. —Psa. 39. 1.

That thy WAY may be known upon earth, thy saving health among all nations.
—Psa. 67. 2.

Thy WAY, O God, is in the sanctuary: who is so great a God as our God? —Psa. 77. 13.

Thy WAY is in the sea, and thy path in the great waters, and thy footsteps are not known. —Psa. 77. 19.

Blessed is the man whose strength is in thee; in whose heart are the WAYS of them.
—Psa. 84. 5.

I will behave myself wisely in a perfect WAY. O when wilt thou come unto me? I will walk within my house with a perfect heart.
—Psa. 101. 2.

He made known his WAYS unto Moses, his acts unto the children of Israel.—Psa. 103. 7.

And he led them forth by the right WAY, that they might go to a city of habitation.
—Psa. 107. 7.

Blessed are the undefiled in the WAY, who walk in the law of the Lord. —Psa. 119. 1.

Wherewithal shall a young man cleanse his WAY? by taking heed thereto according to thy word. —Psa. 119. 9.

I have rejoiced in the WAY of thy testimonies, as much as in all riches. —Psa. 119. 14.

I will meditate in thy precepts, and have respect unto thy WAYS. —Psa. 119. 15.

Make me to understand the WAY of thy precepts: so shall I talk of thy wondrous works.
—Psa. 119. 27.

I will run the WAY of thy commandments, when thou shalt enlarge my heart.—Psa. 119. 32.

Turn away mine eyes from beholding vanity; and quicken thou me in thy WAY.
—Psa. 119. 37.

I thought on my WAYS, and turned my feet unto thy testimonies. —Psa. 119. 59.

I have refrained my feet from every evil WAY, that I might keep thy word.
—Psa. 119. 101.

Through thy precepts I get understanding: therefore I hate every false WAY.
—Psa. 119. 104.

Thy word is a lamp unto my feet, and a light unto my PATH. —Psa. 119. 105.

I esteem all thy precepts concerning all things to be right; and I hate every false WAY.
—Psa. 119. 128.

Blessed is every one that feareth the Lord; that walketh in his WAYS. —Psa. 128. 1.

Yea, they shall sing in the WAYS of the Lord: for great is the glory of the Lord.
—Psa. 138. 5.

Thou compassest my path and my lying down, and art acquainted with all my WAYS.
—Psa. 139. 3.

Lead me in the WAY everlasting.
—Psa. 139. 24.

Cause me to know the WAY wherein I should walk; for I lift up my soul unto thee.
—Psa. 143. 8.

He keepeth the paths of judgment, and preserveth the WAY of his saints. —Prov. 2. 8.

To deliver thee from the WAY of the evil man, from the man that speaketh froward things. —Prov. 2. 12.

That thou mayest walk in the WAY of good men, and keep the paths of the righteous.
—Prov. 2. 20.

In all thy WAYS acknowledge him, and he shall direct thy paths. —Prov. 3. 6.

Her WAYS are WAYS of pleasantness, and all her paths are peace. —Prov. 3. 17.

For the WAYS of man are before the eyes of the Lord, and he pondereth all his goings.
—Prov. 5. 21.

The fear of the Lord is to hate evil: pride, and arrogancy, and the evil WAY. —Prov. 8. 13.

I lead in the WAY of righteousness, in the midst of the paths of judgment. —Prov. 8. 20.

The Lord possessed me in the beginning of his WAY, before his works of old.—Prov. 8. 22.

The wisdom of the prudent is to understand his WAY. —Prov. 14. 8.

The WAY of the righteous is made plain.
—Prov. 15. 19.

When a man's WAYS please the Lord, he maketh even his enemies to be at peace with him. —Prov. 16. 7.

The hoary head is a crown of glory, if it be found in the WAY of righteousness.
—Prov. 16. 31.

Every WAY of a man is right in his own eyes: but the Lord pondereth the hearts.
—Prov. 21. 2.

As for the upright, he directeth his WAY.
—Prov. 21. 29.

Train up a child in the WAY he should go: and when he is old, he will not depart from it.
—Prov. 22. 6.

My son, give me thine heart, and let thine eyes observe my WAYS. —Prov. 23. 26.

She looketh well to the WAYS of her household, and eateth not the bread of idleness. —Prov. 31. 27.

Come ye, and let us go up to the mountain of the Lord, to the house of the God of Jacob; and he will teach us of his WAYS, and we will walk in his paths: for out of Zion shall go forth the law, and the word of the Lord from Jerusalem. —Isa. 2. 3.

The WAY of the just is uprightness: thou, most upright, dost weigh the path of the just. —Isa. 26. 7.

In the WAY of thy judgments, O, Lord, have we waited for thee; the desire of our soul is to thy name, and to the remembrance of thee. —Isa. 26. 8.

And a highWAY shall be there, and a WAY, and it shall be called The WAY of holiness; the unclean shall not pass over it; but it shall be for those: the wayfaring men, though fools, shall not err therein. —Isa. 35. 8.

He pursued them, and passed safely; even by the WAY that he had not gone with his feet. —Isa. 41. 3.

I will bring the blind by a WAY that they knew not; I will lead them in paths that they have not known: I will make darkness light before them, and crooked things straight. These things will I do unto them, and not forsake them. —Isa. 42. 16.

Thus saith the Lord, which maketh a WAY in the sea, and a path in the mighty waters. . . . I will even make a WAY in the wilderness, and rivers in the desert. —Isa. 43. 16, 19.

I have raised him up in righteousness, and I will direct all his WAYS: he shall build my city, and he shall let go my captives, not for prize nor reward, saith the Lord of hosts.
—Isa. 45. 13.

Thus saith the Lord, thy Redeemer, the Holy One of Israel; I am the Lord thy God which teacheth thee to profit, which leadeth thee by the WAY that thou shouldest go.
—Isa. 48. 17.

That thou mayest say to the prisoners, Go forth; to them that are in darkness, Show yourselves. They shall feed in the WAYS, and their pastures shall be in all high places.
—Isa. 49. 9.

They shall not hunger nor thirst; neither shall the heat nor sun smite them: for he that hath mercy on them shall lead them, even by the springs of water shall he guide them. And I will make all my mountains a WAY, and my highWAYS shall be exalted. —Isa. 49. 10, 11.

For my thoughts are not your thoughts, neither are your WAYS my WAYS, saith the Lord. —Isa. 55. 8.

For as the heavens are higher than the earth, so are my WAYS higher than your WAYS, and my thoughts than your thoughts.
—Isa. 55. 9.

Thou art wearied in the greatness of thy WAY; yet saidst thou not, There is no hope: thou hast found the LIFE of thine hand; therefore thou wast not grieved. —Isa. 57. 10.

And shall say, Cast ye up, cast ye up, prepare the WAY, take up the stumbling-block out of the WAY of my people. —Isa. 57. 14.

They seek me daily, and delight to know my WAYS, as a nation that did righteousness.
—Isa. 58. 2.

Thou meetest him that rejoiceth and worketh righteousness, those that remember thee in thy WAYS. —Isa. 64. 5.

I will get me unto the great men, and will speak unto them; for they have known the WAY of the Lord, and the judgment of their God. —Jer. 5. 5.

Thus saith the Lord, Stand ye in the WAYS, and see, and ask for the old paths, where is the good WAY, and walk therein, and ye shall find rest for your souls. —Jer. 6. 16.

I have set thee for a tower and a fortress among my people, that thou mayest know and try their WAY. —Jer. 6. 27.

O Lord, I know that the WAY of man is not in himself: it is not in man that walketh to direct his steps. —Jer. 10. 23.

I the Lord search the heart, I try the reins, even to give every man according to his WAYS, and according to the fruit of his doings. —Jer. 17. 10.

I will cause them to walk by the rivers of waters in a straight WAY, wherein they shall not stumble: for I am a father to Israel.—Jer. 31. 9.

Great in counsel, and mighty in work: for thine eyes are open upon all the WAYS of the sons of men, to give every one according to his WAYS, and according to the fruit of his doings. —Jer. 32. 19.

I will give them one heart, and one WAY, that they may fear me forever, for the good of them, . . . and I will make an everlasting covenant with them. —Jer. 32. 39, 40.

That the Lord thy God may show us the WAY wherein we may walk, and the thing that we may do. —Jer. 42. 3.

They shall ask the WAY to Zion with their faces thitherward, saying, Come, and let us join ourselves to the Lord in a perpetual covenant that shall not be forgotten. —Jer. 50. 5.

And, behold, the glory of the God of Israel came from the WAY of the east: and his voice was like a noise of many waters: and the earth shined with his glory. —Ezek. 43. 2.

Then he brought me back the WAY of the gate of the outward sanctuary which looketh toward the east; and it was shut; . . . because the Lord the God of Israel hath entered in by it. . . . The prince, . . . he shall enter by the WAY, . . . and shall go out by the WAY of the same. Then brought he me the WAY of the north gate. —Ezek. 44. 1-4.

When the prince shall enter, he shall go in by the WAY of the porch of that gate, and he shall go forth by the WAY thereof.—Ezek. 46. 8.

When the people of the land shall come before the Lord in the solemn feasts, he that entereth in by the WAY of the north gate to worship shall go out by the WAY of the south gate; and he that entereth by the WAY of the south gate shall go forth by the WAY of the north gate: he shall not return by the WAY of the gate whereby he came in, but shall go forth over against it. —Ezek. 46. 9.

Then brought he me out of the WAY of the gate northward, and led me about the WAY without unto the outer gate by the WAY that looketh eastward; and, behold, there ran out waters on the right side.
—Ezek. 47. 2.

It was round about eighteen thousand measures: and the name of the city from that day shall be, The Lord is there. —Ezek. 48. 35.

The God in whose hand thy breath is, and whose are all thy WAYS. —Dan. 5. 23.

He said, Go thy WAY, Daniel, . . . till the end be: for thou shalt rest, and stand in thy lot at the end of the days. —Dan. 12. 9, 13.

They shall run like mighty men; they shall climb the wall like men of war; and they shall march every one on his WAYS, and they shall not break their ranks. —Joel 2. 7.

And many nations shall come, and say, Come, and let us go up to the mountain of the Lord, and to the house of the God of Jacob; and he will teach us of his WAYS, and we will walk in his paths: for the law shall go forth of Zion, and the word of the Lord from Jerusalem. —Mic. 4. 2.

The Lord hath his WAY in the whirlwind and in the storm, and the clouds are the dust of his feet. —Nah. 1. 3.

Keep the munition, watch the WAY, make thy loins strong, fortify thy power mightily.
—Nah. 2. 1.

He stood, and measured the earth: he beheld, and drove asunder the nations; and the everlasting mountains were scattered, the perpetual hills did bow: his WAYS are everlasting. —Hab. 3. 6.

Now therefore thus saith the Lord of hosts; Consider your WAYS. —Hag. 1. 5.

The pillar of  the cloud departed not from them by day, to lead them in the WAY; neither the pillar of fire by night, to show them light, and the WAY wherein they should go. —Neh. 9. 19.

And a highWAY shall be there, and a WAY, and it shall be called The WAY of holiness; the unclean shall not pass over it; but it shall be for those: the wayfaring men, though fools, shall not err therein. —Isa. 35. 8.

The voice of him that crieth in the wilderness, Prepare ye the WAY of the Lord, make straight in the desert a highWAY for our God.
—Isa. 40. 3.

Behold, I will send my messenger, and he shall prepare the WAY before me: and the Lord, whom ye seek, shall suddenly come to his temple, even the messenger of the covenant, whom ye delight in: behold, he shall come, saith the Lord of hosts. —Mal. 3. 1.

In those days came John the Baptist, preaching in the wilderness of Judea, and saying, Repent ye: for the kingdom of heaven is at hand. For this is he that was spoken of by the prophet Esaias, saying, The voice of one crying in the wilderness, Prepare ye the WAY of the Lord, make his paths straight.
—Matt. 3. 1-3.

Jesus himself drew near, and went with them. —Luke 24. 15.

And they said one to another, Did not our heart burn within us, while he talked with us by the WAY, and while he opened to us the Scriptures? —Luke 24. 32.

And they told what things were done in the WAY. —Luke 24. 35.

And he said unto them, These are the words which I spake unto you, . . . that all things must be fulfilled, which were written in the law of Moses, and in the prophets, and in the psalms, concerning me. —Luke 24. 44.

New Testament.

And being warned of God in a dream that they should not return to Herod, they departed into their own country another WAY.
—Matt. 2. 12.

Leave there thy gift before the altar, and go thy WAY; first be reconciled to thy brother, and then come and offer thy gift. —Matt. 5. 24.

Agree with thine adversary quickly, while thou art in the WAY. —Matt. 5. 25.

Because strait is the gate, and narrow is the WAY, which leadeth unto LIFE.—Matt. 7. 14.

Go thy WAY, show thyself to the priest.
—Matt. 8. 4.

And Jesus said unto the centurion, Go thy WAY; and as thou hast believed, so be it done unto thee. —Matt. 8. 13.

Then Jesus called his disciples unto him, and said, I have compassion on the multitude, because they continue with me now three days, and have nothing to eat: and I will not send them away fasting, lest they faint in the WAY. —Matt. 15. 32.

Go ye also into the vineyard, and whatsoever is right I will give you. And they went their WAY. —Matt. 20. 4.

Take that thine is, and go thy WAY.
—Matt. 20. 14.

And a very great multitude spread their garments in the WAY; others cut down branches from the trees, and strewed them in the WAY. —Matt. 21. 8.

Saying, Master, we know that thou art true, and teachest the WAY of God in TRUTH.
—Matt. 22. 16.

For this saying go thy WAY; the devil is gone out of thy daughter. —Mark 7. 29.

By the WAY he asked his disciples, saying unto them, whom do men say that I am? . . . And Peter answereth and saith unto him, Thou art the Christ. Mark 8. 27, 29.

Then Jesus beholding him loved him, and said unto him, one thing thou lackest: go thy

WAY, sell whatsoever thou hast, and give to the poor, and thou shalt have treasure in heaven: and come, take up the cross, and follow me. —Mark 10. 21.

And they were in the WAY going up to Jerusalem; and Jesus went before them.
—Mark 10. 32.

And Jesus said unto him, Go thy WAY; thy faith hath made thee whole. And immediately he received his sight, and followed Jesus in the WAY. —Mark 10. 52.

And saith unto them, Go your WAY into the village over against you: and as soon as ye be entered into it, ye shall find a colt tied, whereon never man sat; loose him, and bring him. . . . And they went their WAY, and found the colt tied by the door without in a place where two WAYS met. . . . And many spread their garments in the WAY.
—Mark 11. 2-8.

And when they were come, they say unto him, Master, we know that thou art true, and carest for no man; for thou regardest not the person of men, but teachest the WAY of God in TRUTH. —Mark 12. 14.

And when the sabbath was past, Mary Magdalene, and Mary the mother of James, and Salome, had brought sweet spices, that they might come and anoint him. . . . He saith unto them, . . . Go your WAY, tell his disciples and Peter that he goeth before you into Galilee: there shall ye see him, as he said unto you. —Mark 16. 1-7.

And thou, child, shalt be called the prophet of the Highest: for thou shalt go before the face of the Lord to prepare his WAYS. —Luke 1. 76.

To guide our feet into the WAY of peace. —Luke 1. 79.

Jesus answering said unto them, Go your WAY, and tell John what things ye have seen and heard; how that the blind see, the lame walk, the lepers are cleansed, the deaf hear, the dead are raised, to the poor the gospel is preached. —Luke 7. 22.

Jesus sent him away, saying, Return to thine own house, and show how great things God

hath done unto thee. And he went his WAY, and published throughout the whole city how great things Jesus had done unto him.
—Luke 8. 38, 39.

It came to pass, that, as they went in the WAY, a certain man said unto him, Lord, I will follow thee whithersoever thou goest.
—Luke 9. 57.

Or else, while the other is yet a great WAY off, he sendeth an embassage, and desireth conditions of peace. —Luke 14. 32.

Jesus answering said, Were there not ten cleansed? but where are the nine? There are not found that returned to give glory to God, save this stranger. And he said unto him, Arise, go thy WAY: thy faith hath made thee whole. —Luke 17. 17-19.

It came to pass, that as he was come nigh unto Jericho, a certain blind man sat by the WAY-side begging: and hearing the multitude pass by, he asked what it meant. And they told him that Jesus of Nazareth passeth by. —Luke 18. 35-37.

And they that were sent went their WAY, and found even as he had said unto them. . . . And as he went, they spread their clothes in the WAY. . . . Saying, Blessed be the king that cometh in the name of the Lord: peace in heaven, and glory in the highest.

—Luke 19. 32-38.

Master, we know that thou sayest and teachest rightly, neither acceptest thou the person of any, but teachest the WAY of God truly.

—Luke 20. 21.

The woman then left her water-pot, and went her WAY into the city, and saith to the men, Come, see a man, which told me all things that ever I did: is not this the Christ?—John 4. 28, 29.

Jesus saith unto him, Go thy WAY; thy son liveth. And the man believed the word that Jesus had spoken unto him, and he went his WAY. —John 4. 50.

Then said Jesus again unto them, I go my WAY. —John 8. 21.

And as Jesus passed by, he saw a man which was blind from his birth. . . . And said unto him, Go, wash in the pool of Siloam. . . . He went his WAY therefore, and washed, and came seeing. —John 9. 1-7.

But now I go my WAY to him that sent me.
—John 16. 5.

Thou hast made known to me the WAYS of life; thou shalt make me full of joy with thy countenance. —Acts 2. 28.

The angel of the Lord spake unto Philip, saying, Arise, and go toward the south, unto the WAY that goeth down from Jerusalem unto Gaza. —Acts 8. 26.

Then Philip opened his mouth, and began at the same Scripture, and preached unto him Jesus. . . . As they went on their WAY. . . . And when they were come up out of the water, the Spirit of the Lord caught away Philip, that the eunuch saw him no more: and he went on his WAY rejoicing. —Acts 8. 35-39.

But the Lord said unto him, Go thy WAY: for he is a chosen vessel unto me. . . . And Ananias went his WAY, and entered into the house; and putting his hands on him said,

Brother Saul, the Lord, even Jesus, that appeared unto thee in the WAY. . . . But Barnabas took him, and brought him to the apostles, and declared unto them how he had seen the Lord in the WAY, and that he had spoken to him. —Acts 9. 15-27.

And a certain Jew named Apollos, born at Alexandria, an eloquent man, and mighty in the Scriptures, came to Ephesus. This man was instructed in the WAY of the Lord. . . . And he began to speak boldly in the synagogue: whom when Aquila and Priscilla had heard, they took him unto them, and expounded unto him the WAY of God more perfectly. —Acts 18. 24-26.

Who said to Paul through the Spirit, that he should not go up to Jerusalem. And when we had accomplished those days, we departed and went our WAY; and they all brought us on our WAY, with wives and children, till we were out of the city: and we kneeled down on the shore, and prayed. —Acts 21. 4, 5.

What advantage then hath the Jew? . . .
Much every WAY : chiefly, because that unto
them were committed the oracles of God.
—Rom. 3. 1, 2.

O the depth of the riches both of the wisdom
and knowledge of God! how unsearchable are
his judgments, and his WAYS past finding out.
—Rom. 11. 33.

For this cause have I sent unto you Timotheus, who is my beloved son, and faithful in the Lord, who shall bring you into remembrance of my WAYS which be in Christ, as I teach every-where in every church.—1 Cor. 4. 17.

There hath no temptation taken you but such as is common to man : but God is faithful, who will not suffer you to be tempted above that ye are able ; but will with the temptation also make a WAY to escape, that ye may be able to bear it.
—1 Cor. 10. 13.

For I will not see you now by the WAY ; but I trust to tarry a while with you, if the Lord permit. —1 Cor. 16. 7.

To pass by you into Macedonia, and to come again out of Macedonia unto you, and of you to be brought on my WAY toward Judea. —2 Cor. 1. 16.

Now God himself and our Father, and our Lord Jesus Christ, direct our WAY.
—1 Thess. 3. 11.

The Holy Ghost this signifying, that the WAY into the holiest of all was not yet made manifest, while as the first tabernacle was yet standing. —Heb. 9. 8.

Having therefore, brethren, boldness to enter into the holiest by the blood of Jesus, by a new and living WAY, which he hath consecrated for us, through the vail, that is to say, his flesh ; and having a high-priest over the house of God.
—Heb. 10. 19-21.

And make straight paths for your feet, lest that which is lame be turned out of the WAY; but let it rather be healed. —Heb. 12. 13.

They sing the song of Moses the servant of God, and the song of the Lamb, saying, Great and marvelous are thy works, Lord God Almighty; just and true are thy WAYS, thou King of saints. —Rev. 15. 3.

PROLUSION.

DEFINITION OF

By NOAH WEBSTER, LL.D.

ONE. The quality of being true. Conformity to fact or reality. Exact accordance with that which is, or has been, or shall be. Conformity to rule; exactness; close correspondence with an example, model, object of imitation, or the like. Fidelity; constancy.

Plows, to go true, depend much on the TRUTH of the iron-work.—MORTIMER.

> Alas! they had been friends in youth,
> But whispering tongues can poison TRUTH.
> —COLERIDGE.

The practice of speaking TRUTH; habitual disposition to speak TRUTH; freedom from falsehood; veracity; as, he is a man of TRUTH. Honesty; virtue.

> It must appear
> That malice bears down TRUTH.—SHAK.

2. That which is true or certain concerning any matter or subject, or generally on all subjects; real state of things; verity; reality.

I long to know the TRUTH hereof at large.—SHAK.

The TRUTH depends on, or is only arrived at by, a legitimate deduction from all the facts which are truly material.—COLERIDGE.

3. A true thing; a verified fact; a true statement or proposition; an established principle, fixed law, or the like; as, the great TRUTHS of morals.

My mouth shall speak TRUTH.—PROV. 8. 7.

Sanctify them through thy TRUTH; thy word is TRUTH.—JOHN 17. 17.

In TRUTH, in reality; in fact.—Of a TRUTH, in reality; certainly.—To do TRUTH, to practice what God commands.

TRUTH. To assert as true; to declare.

Had they dreamt this, they would have TRUTHED it
        heaven.—FORD.

TRUE. 1. Conformable to fact; in accordance with the actual state of things; not false, erroneous, inaccurate, or the like; as, a TRUE relation or narration;

a TRUE history; a declaration is TRUE when it states the facts. In this sense, TRUE is opposed to false.

'Tis very TRUE, O wise and upright judge.—SHAK.

2. Right to precision; conformable to a rule or pattern; exact; as, a TRUE copy; a TRUE likeness of the original.

Thus did he maintain the defensive, making his eye, foot, and hand keep TRUE time.—W. SCOTT.

3. Steady in adhering to friends, to promises, to a prince, or the like; faithful; loyal; not false, fickle, or perfidious; as, a TRUE friend; a wife TRUE to her husband; an officer TRUE to his charge.

Thy so TRUE,
So faithful love unequaled.—MILTON.

Dare to be TRUE; nothing can need a lie.—HERBERT.

4. Actual; not counterfeit, adulterated, or pretended; genuine; pure; real; as, TRUE balsam; TRUE love of country; a TRUE Christian.

The TRUE light, which lighteth every man that cometh into the world.—ST. JOHN I. 9.

Not myself, but the TRUTH that in LIFE I
    have spoken,
  Not myself, but the seed that in LIFE I
    have sown,
Shall pass on to ages—all about me forgotten,
  Save the TRUTH I have spoken, the things
    I have done.   —Bonar.

TRUTH.

I AM the DOOR: by me if any man enter in, he shall be saved, and shall go in and out, and find pasture. —John 10. 9.

When quiet in my house I sit,
   Thy book be my companion still;
My joy thy sayings to repeat,
   Talk o'er the records of thy will,
And search the oracles divine,
Till every heart-felt word be mine.
—Charles Wesley.

Let us not love in word, neither in tongue; but in deed and in TRUTH. —1 John 3. 18.

Source of TRUTH, whose beams alone
   Light the mighty world of mind;
God of love, who from thy throne,
   Kindly watchest all mankind.
—William Cullen Bryant.

Marble and recording brass decay,
And like the graver's memory pass away;
The works of man inherit, as is just,
Their author's frailty, and return to dust;
But TRUTH divine forever stands secure:
Fixed is the rolling flood of endless years;
The Pillar of the eternal plan appears;
The raving storm and dashing wave defies,
Built by that Architect who built the skies.
—Cowper.

Careless seems the great avenger:
   History's pages but record
One death-grapple in the darkness
   'Twixt old systems and the Word.
TRUTH forever on the scaffold,
   Wrong forever on the throne;
Yet that scaffold sways the future,
   And behind the dim unknown
Standeth God within the shadow,
   Keeping watch above his own.
—Lowell.

TRUTH is as impossible to be soiled by any outward touch as the sunbeam. —Milton.

TRUTH crushed to earth shall rise again:
The eternal years of God are hers. —Bryant.

TRUTH against the world. —Tennyson.

Though all the winds of doctrine were let loose to play upon earth, so TRUTH be in the field, we do ingloriously, by licensing and prohibiting, to misdoubt her strength. Let her and falsehood grapple: who ever knew TRUTH put to the worse in a free and open encounter? —Milton.

Infinite TRUTH, the LIFE of my desire,
Come from the skies and join thyself to me;
I am tired with hearing, and this hearing tires,
But never tired of telling thee
'Tis thy fair face alone my spirit burns to see.
—Isaac Watts.

O TRUTH, TRUTH! thou knowest how the inward marrow of my soul longeth after thee. —Augustine.

Great TRUTHS are portions of the soul of man;
Great souls are portions of eternity. —Lowell.

The entrance of thy words giveth light; it giveth understanding. —Psa. 119. 130.

I will show thee that which is noted in the Scripture of TRUTH. —Dan. 10. 21.

Thou wilt perform the TRUTH to Jacob, and the mercy to Abraham, which thou hast sworn unto our fathers from the days of old.
—Mic. 7. 20.

Come Holy Guest, for moved by thee
    The prophets wrote and spoke,
Unlock the TRUTH, thyself the key;
    Unseal the sacred book. —Charles Wesley.

And now I will show thee the TRUTH.
—Dan. 11. 2.

Old Testament.

Blessed be the Lord God of my master Abraham, who hath not left destitute my master of his mercy and his TRUTH.
—Gen. 24. 27.

[Jacob said] I am not worthy of the least of all the mercies, and of all the TRUTH, which thou hast showed unto thy servant.
—Gen. 32. 10.

And Joseph said unto them, . . . Hereby ye shall be proved. . . . Send one of you, and . . . fetch your brother, . . . that your words may be proved, whether there be any TRUTH in you.
—Gen. 42. 14-16.

Moreover thou shalt provide out of all the people able men, such as fear God, men of TRUTH, hating covetousness.
—Exod. 18. 21.

And the Lord passed by before him, and proclaimed, The Lord, The Lord God, merciful and gracious, long-suffering, and abundant in goodness and TRUTH.
—Exod. 34. 6.

Then shalt thou inquire, and make search, and ask diligently; and, behold, if it be TRUTH, and the thing certain. —Deut. 13. 14.

He is the Rock, his work is perfect: for all his WAYS are judgment: a God of TRUTH and without iniquity, just and right is he.
—Deut. 32. 4.

Only fear the Lord, and serve him in TRUTH with all your heart: for consider how great things he hath done for you.
—1 Sam. 12. 24.

And Joshua said unto all the people, . . . Now therefore fear the Lord, and serve him in sincerity and in TRUTH. . . . As for me and my house, we will serve the Lord.
—Josh. 24. 2, 14, 15.

And now the Lord show kindness and TRUTH unto you: and I also will requite you this kindness, because ye have done this thing. —2 Sam. 2. 6.

That the Lord may continue his word which he spake concerning me, saying, If thy children take heed to their WAY, to walk before me in TRUTH with all their heart, . . . there shall not fail thee (said he) a man on the throne of Israel. —1 Kings 2. 4.

And the woman said to Elijah, Now by this I know that thou art a man of God, and that the word of the Lord in thy mouth is TRUTH.
—1 Kings 17. 24.

Of a TRUTH, Lord, the kings of Assyria have destroyed the nations and their lands.
—2 Kings 19. 17.

I beseech thee, O Lord, remember now how I have walked before thee in TRUTH and with a perfect heart, and have done . . . good in thy sight. And Hezekiah wept sore. And he said, Is it not good, if peace and TRUTH be in my days? —2 Kings 20. 3, 19.

And the king said to him, How many times shall I adjure thee that thou say nothing but the TRUTH to me in the name of the Lord? —2 Chron. 18. 15.

And thus did Hezekiah throughout all Judah, and wrought that which was good and right and TRUTH before the Lord his God.
—2 Chron. 31. 20.

And he sent the letters unto all the Jews, to the hundred twenty and seven provinces of the kingdom of Ahasuerus, with words of peace and TRUTH. —Esth. 9. 30.

Then Job answered and said, I know it is so of a TRUTH: but how should man be just with God? —Job 9. 1, 2.

He that walketh uprightly, and worketh righteousness, and speaketh the TRUTH in his heart. —Psa. 15. 2.

Lead me in thy TRUTH, and teach me: for thou art the God of my salvation. All the paths of the Lord are mercy and TRUTH unto such as keep his covenant and his testimonies. —Psa. 25. 5, 10.

For thy loving-kindness is before mine eyes: and I have walked in thy TRUTH.
—Psa. 26. 3.

Shall the dust praise thee? shall it declare thy TRUTH? —Psa. 30. 9.

Into thine hand I commit my spirit: thou hast redeemed me, O Lord God of TRUTH.
—Psa. 31. 5.

For the word of the Lord is right; and all his works are done in TRUTH. —Psa. 33. 4.

I have not hid thy righteousness within my heart; I have declared thy faithfulness and thy salvation: I have not concealed thy loving-kindness and thy TRUTH from the great congregation. . . . Let thy loving-kindness and thy TRUTH continually preserve me.
—Psa. 40. 10, 11.

O send out thy light and thy TRUTH: let them lead me; let them bring me unto thy holy hill. —Psa. 43. 3.

And in thy majesty ride prosperously, because of TRUTH and meekness and righteousness. —Psa. 45. 4.

Behold, thou desirest TRUTH, . . . in the hidden part thou shalt make me to know wisdom. —Psa. 51. 6.

He shall reward evil unto mine enemies: cut them off in thy TRUTH. —Psa. 54. 5.

God shall send forth his mercy and his TRUTH. For thy mercy is great unto the heavens, and thy TRUTH unto the clouds.
—Psa. 57. 3, 10.

He shall abide before God forever: O prepare mercy and TRUTH, which may preserve him.
—Psa. 61. 7.

O God, in the multitude of thy mercy hear me, in the TRUTH of thy salvation.
—Psa. 69. 13.

I will also praise thee with the psaltery, even thy TRUTH, O my God: unto thee will I sing with the harp, O thou Holy One of Israel.
—Psa. 71. 22.

Mercy and TRUTH are met together; righteousness and peace have kissed each other. TRUTH shall spring out of the earth; and righteousness shall look down from heaven.
—Psa. 85. 10, 11.

Teach me thy WAY, O Lord; I will walk in thy TRUTH: unite my heart to fear thy name.
—Psa. 86. 11.

Justice and judgment are the habitation of thy throne: mercy and TRUTH shall go before thy face. Lord, where are thy former loving-kindnesses, which thou swarest unto David in thy TRUTH? —Psa. 89. 14, 49.

He shall judge the world with righteousness, and the people with his TRUTH.—Psa. 96. 13.

He hath remembered his mercy and his TRUTH toward the house of Israel.—Psa. 98. 3.

For the Lord is good; his mercy is everlasting; and his TRUTH endureth to all generations. —Psa. 100. 5.

For thy mercy is great above the heavens: and thy TRUTH reacheth unto the clouds.
—Psa. 108. 4.

They stand fast for ever and ever, and are done in TRUTH and uprightness.—Psa. 111. 8.

Not unto us, O Lord, not unto us, but unto thy name give glory, for thy mercy, and for thy TRUTH'S sake. —Psa. 115. 1.

O praise the Lord, all ye nations: praise him, all ye people. For his merciful kindness is great toward us: and the TRUTH of the Lord endureth forever. —Psa. 117. 1, 2.

I have chosen the WAY of TRUTH: thy judgments have I laid before me. And take not the word of TRUTH utterly out of my mouth. Thy righteousness is an everlasting righteousness, and thy law is the TRUTH. Thou art near, O Lord; and all thy commandments are TRUTH. —Psa. 119. 30, 43, 142, 151.

The Lord hath sworn in TRUTH unto David; he will not turn from it. —Psa. 132. 11.

I will worship toward thy holy temple, and praise thy name for thy loving-kindness and for thy TRUTH: for thou hast magnified thy word above all thy name. —Psa. 138. 2.

Which made heaven, and earth, the sea, and all that therein is: which keepeth TRUTH forever. —Psa. 146. 6.

Let not mercy and TRUTH forsake thee: bind them about thy neck; write them upon the table of thine heart. —Prov. 3. 3.

For my mouth shall speak TRUTH; and wickedness is an abomination to my lips.
—Prov. 8. 7.

He that speaketh TRUTH showeth forth righteousness. The lip of TRUTH shall be established forever. —Prov. 12. 17, 19.

Mercy and TRUTH shall be to them that devise good. —Prov. 14. 22.

By mercy and TRUTH iniquity is purged: and by the fear of the Lord men depart from evil. —Prov. 16. 6.

Mercy and TRUTH preserve the king: and his throne is upholden by mercy. —Prov. 20. 28.

That I might make thee know the certainty of the words of TRUTH; that thou mightest answer the words of TRUTH to them that send unto thee? —Prov. 22. 21.

Buy the TRUTH, and sell it not; also wisdom, and instruction, and understanding.
—Prov. 23. 23.

And it shall come to pass in that day, that the remnant of Israel, and such as are escaped of the house of Jacob, shall no more again stay upon him that smote them; but shall stay upon the Lord, the Holy One of Israel, in TRUTH.
—Isa. 10. 20.

In mercy shall the throne be established: and he shall sit upon it in TRUTH in the tabernacle of David, judging, and seeking judgment, and hasting righteousness. —Isa. 16. 5.

O Lord, thou art my God; I will exalt thee, I will praise thy name; for thou hast done wonderful things; thy counsels of old are faithfulness and TRUTH. —Isa. 25. 1.

In that day shall this song be sung in the land of Judah; We have a strong city; salvation will God appoint for walls and bulwarks. Open ye the gates, that the righteous nation which keepeth the TRUTH may enter in.
—Isa. 26. 1, 2.

Of a TRUTH, Lord, the kings of Assyria have laid waste all the nations, and their countries. —Isa. 37. 18.

Then Hezekiah turned his face toward the wall, and prayed unto the Lord, and said, Remember now, O Lord, I beseech thee, how I have walked before thee in TRUTH and with a perfect heart, and have done that which is good in thy sight. They that go down into the pit cannot hope for thy TRUTH. The living, the living, he shall praise thee, as I do this day: the father to the children shall make known thy TRUTH. —Isa. 38. 2, 3, 18, 19.

Then said Hezekiah to Isaiah, Good is the word of the Lord which thou hast spoken. He said moreover, For there shall be peace and TRUTH in my days. —Isa. 39. 8.

A bruised reed shall he not break, and the smoking flax shall he not quench: he shall bring forth judgment unto TRUTH.
—Isa. 42. 3.

Let them bring forth their witnesses, that they may be justified: or let them hear, and say, It is TRUTH. —Isa. 43. 9.

Hear ye this, O house of Jacob, which are called by the name of Israel, and are come forth out of the waters of Judah, which swear by the name of the Lord, and make mention of the God of Israel, but not in TRUTH, nor in righteousness. —Isa. 48. 1.

None calleth for justice, nor any pleadeth for TRUTH. And judgment is turned away backward, and justice standeth afar off: for TRUTH is fallen in the street, and equity cannot enter. Yea, TRUTH faileth.
—Isa. 59. 4, 14, 15.

For I the Lord love judgment, I hate robbery for burnt-offering; and I will direct their work in TRUTH, and I will make an everlasting covenant with them. —Isa. 61. 8.

That he who blesseth himself in the earth shall bless himself in the God of TRUTH; and he that sweareth in the earth shall swear by the God of TRUTH. —Isa. 65. 16.

Thou shalt swear, The Lord liveth, in TRUTH, in judgment, and in righteousness.
—Jer. 4. 2.

Run ye to and fro through the streets of Jerusalem, and see now, and know, and seek in the broad places thereof, if ye can find a man, if there be any that executeth judgment, that seeketh the TRUTH. —Jer. 5. 1.

TRUTH is perished, and is cut off from their mouth. —Jer. 7. 28.

For of a TRUTH the Lord hath sent me unto you to speak all these words in your ears.
—Jer. 26. 15.

Behold, I will bring it health and cure, and I will cure them, and will reveal unto them the abundance of peace and TRUTH.
—Jer. 33. 6.

The king answered unto Daniel, and said, Of a TRUTH it is, that your God is a God of gods, and a Lord of kings, and a revealer of secrets, seeing thou couldest reveal this secret.
—Dan. 2. 47.

Now I Nebuchadnezzar praise and extol and honor the King of heaven, all whose works are TRUTH, and his WAYS judgment.
—Dan. 4. 37.

By reason of transgression, . . . it cast down the TRUTH to the ground. —Dan. 8. 12.

That we might turn from our iniquities, and understand thy TRUTH. —Dan. 9. 13.

For the Lord hath a controversy with the

inhabitants of the land, because there is no TRUTH, nor mercy, nor knowledge of God in the land. —Hos. 4. 1.

Jerusalem shall be called A city of TRUTH; and the mountain of the Lord of hosts, The holy mountain. They shall be my people, and I will be their God, in TRUTH and in righteousness. These are the things that ye shall do; Speak ye every man the TRUTH to his neighbor; execute the judgment of TRUTH and peace in your gates. Joy and gladness, and cheerful feasts; therefore love the TRUTH and peace. —Zech. 8. 3, 8, 16, 19.

The law of TRUTH was in his mouth, and iniquity was not found in his lips: he walked with me in peace and equity, and did turn many away from iniquity. —Mal. 2. 6.

Happy is he whom TRUTH by itself doth teach. —Thomas à Kempis.

TRUTH is the property of God; the pursuit of TRUTH belongs to man. —Von Muller.

And they sung a new song, saying, Thou art worthy to take the Book, and to open the seals thereof. —Rev. 5. 9.

The Preacher sought to find out acceptable words: and that which was written was upright, even words of TRUTH. —Eccl. 12. 10.

When the majestic form of TRUTH approaches, bow and obey. —John Foster.

Hark, hark, my soul! angelic songs are swelling
  O'er earth's green fields and ocean's wave-beat shore :
How sweet the TRUTH those blessed strains are telling
  Of that new LIFE when sin shall be no more!
    Angels of Jesus, angels of light,
    Singing to welcome the pilgrims of the night! —F. W. Faber.

New Testament.

Then they that were in the ship came and worshiped him, saying, Of a TRUTH thou art the Son of God. —Matt. 14. 33.

And she said, TRUTH, Lord: yet the dogs eat of the crumbs which fall from their masters' table. —Matt. 15. 27.

And he looked round about to see her that had done this thing. But the woman fearing and trembling, knowing what was done in her, came and fell down before him, and told him all the TRUTH. —Mark 5. 32, 33.

And when they were come, they say unto him, Master, we know that thou art TRUE, and carest for no man; for thou regardest not the person of men, but teachest the WAY of God in TRUTH: Is it lawful to give tribute to Cæsar, or not? And the scribe said unto him, Well, Master, thou hast said the TRUTH: for there is one God; and there is none other but he. —Mark 12. 14, 32.

I tell you of a TRUTH, many widows were in Israel in the days of Elias, when the heaven was shut up three years and six months, when great famine was throughout all the land.
—Luke 4. 25.

I tell you of a TRUTH, there be some standing here, which shall not taste of death, till they see the kingdom of God. —Luke 9. 27.

Of a TRUTH I say unto you, that he will make him ruler over all that he hath.
—Luke 12. 44.

And he said, Of a TRUTH I say unto you, that this poor widow hath cast in more than they all. —Luke 21. 3.

And about the space of one hour after another confidently affirmed, saying, Of a TRUTH this fellow also was with him; for he is a Galilean. —Luke 22. 59.

And the Word was made flesh, and dwelt among us, (and we beheld his glory, the glory as of the only-begotten of the Father,) full of grace and TRUTH. For the law was given by Moses, but grace and TRUTH came by Jesus Christ. —John 1. 14, 17.

But he that doeth TRUTH cometh to the light, that his deeds may be made manifest, that they are wrought in God. He that hath received his testimony hath set to his seal that God is TRUE. —John 3. 21, 33.

The hour cometh, and now is, when the TRUE worshipers shall worship the Father in spirit and in TRUTH: for the Father seeketh such to worship him. God is a Spirit: and they that worship him must worship him in spirit and in TRUTH. —John 4. 23, 24.

If I bear witness of myself, my witness is not TRUE. There is another that beareth witness of me; and I know that the witness which he witnesseth of me is TRUE. Ye sent unto John, and he bare witness unto the TRUTH. —John 5. 31-33.

Then those men, when they had seen the miracle that Jesus did, said, This is of a TRUTH that Prophet that should come into the world. —John 6. 14.

Many of the people therefore, when they heard this saying, said, Of a TRUTH this is the Prophet. —John 7. 40.

[Jesus said] If ye continue in my word, then are ye my disciples indeed; and ye shall know the TRUTH, and the TRUTH shall make you free. But now ye seek to kill me, a man that hath told you the TRUTH, which I have heard of God: this did not Abraham. Ye are of your father the devil, and the lusts of your father ye will do: he was a murderer from the beginning, and abode not in the TRUTH, because there is no TRUTH in him. When he speaketh a lie, he speaketh of his own: for he is a liar, and the father of it. And because I tell you the TRUTH, ye believe me not. Which of you convinceth me of sin? And if I say the TRUTH, why do ye not believe me? —John 8. 31, 32, 40, 44, 45, 46.

If ye love me, keep my commandments. And I will pray the Father, and he shall give you another Comforter, that he may abide with you forever; even the Spirit of TRUTH; whom the world cannot receive, because it seeth him not, neither knoweth him: but ye know him; for he dwelleth with you, and shall be in you. —John 14. 15-17.

But when the Comforter is come, whom I will send unto you from the Father, even the Spirit of TRUTH, which proceedeth from the Father, he shall testify of me. —John 15. 26.

Nevertheless I tell you the TRUTH; It is expedient for you that I go away: for if I go not away, the Comforter will not come unto you; but if I depart, I will send him unto you. Howbeit when he, the Spirit of TRUTH, is come, he will guide you into all TRUTH: for he shall not speak of himself; but whatsoever he shall hear, that shall he speak: and he will show you things to come. —John 16. 7, 13.

Sanctify them through thy TRUTH: thy word is TRUTH. And for their sakes I sanctify myself, that they also might be sanctified through the TRUTH. —John 17. 17, 19.

Pilate therefore said unto him, Art thou a king then? Jesus answered, Thou sayest that I am a king. To this end was I born, and for this cause came I into the world, that I should bear witness unto the TRUTH. Every one that is of the TRUTH heareth my voice. Pilate saith unto him, What is TRUTH?
—John 18. 37, 38.

For of a TRUTH against thy holy child Jesus, whom thou hast anointed. —Acts 4. 27.

Then Peter opened his mouth, and said, Of a TRUTH I perceive that God is no respecter of persons: but in every nation he that feareth him, and worketh righteousness, is accepted with him. —Acts 10. 34, 35.

He [Paul] said, I am not mad, most noble Festus; but speak forth the words of TRUTH and soberness. —Acts 26. 25.

For the wrath of God is revealed from heaven against all ungodliness and unrighteousness of men, who hold the TRUTH in unrighteousness; who changed the TRUTH of God into

a lie, and worshiped and served the creature more than the Creator, who is blessed forever.
—Rom. 1. 18, 25.

But we are sure that the judgment of God is according to TRUTH against them which commit such things. But unto them that are contentious, and do not obey the TRUTH, but obey unrighteousness, indignation and wrath. An instructor of the foolish, a teacher of babes, which hast the form of knowledge and of the TRUTH in the law. —Rom. 2. 2, 8, 20.

For if the TRUTH of God hath more abounded through my lie unto his glory; why yet am I also judged as a sinner? —Rom. 3. 7.

I say that Jesus Christ was a minister of the circumcision for the TRUTH of God, to confirm the promises made unto the fathers.
—Rom. 15. 8.

Therefore let us keep the feast, not with old leaven, neither with the leaven of malice and wickedness; but with the unleavened bread of sincerity and TRUTH. —1 Cor. 5. 8.

Rejoiceth not in iniquity, but rejoiceth in the TRUTH. —1 Cor. 13. 6.

And thus are the secrets of his heart made manifest; and so falling down on his face he will worship God, and report that God is in you of a TRUTH. —1 Cor. 14. 25.

By manifestation of the TRUTH, commending ourselves to every man's conscience in the sight of God. —2 Cor. 4. 2.

By the word of TRUTH, by the power of God, by the armor of righteousness on the right hand and on the left. —2 Cor. 6. 7.

But as we spake all things to you in TRUTH, even so our boasting, which I made before Titus, is found a TRUTH.—2 Cor. 7. 14.

As the TRUTH of Christ is in me.
—2 Cor. 11. 10.

For I will say the TRUTH. —2 Cor. 12. 6.

We can do nothing against the TRUTH, but for the TRUTH. —2 Cor. 13. 8.

That the TRUTH of the gospel might continue with you. I saw that they walked not uprightly according to the TRUTH of the gospel. —Gal. 2. 5, 14.

Who hath bewitched you, that ye should not obey the TRUTH, before whose eyes Jesus Christ hath been evidently set forth.
—Gal. 3. 1.

Am I therefore become your enemy, because I tell you the TRUTH. —Gal. 4. 16.

Ye did run well; who did hinder you that ye should not obey the TRUTH? —Gal. 5. 7.

In whom ye also trusted, after that ye heard the word of TRUTH, the gospel of your salvation: in whom also, after that ye believed, ye were sealed with that Holy Spirit of promise, which is the earnest of our inheritance.
—Eph. 1. 13, 14.

But speaking the TRUTH in love, may grow up into him in all things, which is the head, even Christ. If so be that ye have heard him, and have been taught by him, as the TRUTH is in Jesus. And . . . put on the new man, which after God is created in righteousness and TRUE holiness. Wherefore putting away lying, speak every man TRUTH with his neighbor: for we are members one of another. —Eph. 4. 15, 21, 24, 25.

(For the fruit of the Spirit is in all goodness and righteousness and TRUTH;) proving what is acceptable unto the Lord.
—Eph. 5. 9, 10.

Stand therefore, having your loins girt about with TRUTH, and having on the breastplate of righteousness. —Eph. 6. 14.

I am set for the defense of the gospel. What then? notwithstanding, every WAY, whether in pretense, or in TRUTH, Christ is preached; and I therein do rejoice, yea, and will rejoice. —Phil. 1. 17, 18.

For the hope which is laid up for you in heaven, whereof ye heard before in the word of the TRUTH of the gospel; which is come unto you, as it is in all the world; and bringeth forth fruit, as it doth also in you, since the day ye heard of it, and knew the grace of God in TRUTH. —Col. 1. 5, 6.

For this cause also thank we God without ceasing, because, when ye received the word of God which ye heard of us, ye received it not as the word of men, but, as it is in TRUTH, the word of God, which effectually worketh also in you that believe. —1 Thess. 2. 13.

Because they received not the love of the TRUTH, that they might be saved. That they all might be damned who believed not the TRUTH, but had pleasure in unrighteousness. But we are bound to give thanks always to God for you, brethren beloved of the Lord, because God hath from the beginning chosen you to salvation through sanctification of the Spirit and belief of the TRUTH.
—2 Thess. 2. 10, 12, 13.

Who will have all men to be saved, and to come unto the knowledge of the TRUTH. Whereunto I am ordained a preacher, and an apostle, (I speak the TRUTH in Christ, and lie not,) a teacher of the Gentiles in faith and verity. —1 Tim. 2. 4, 7.

Which is the church of the living God, the pillar and ground of the TRUTH. To be received with thanksgiving of them which believe and know the TRUTH.—1 Tim. 3. 15; 4. 3.

Perverse disputings of men of corrupt minds, and destitute of the TRUTH, supposing that gain is godliness: from such withdraw thyself.
—1 Tim. 6. 5.

Who concerning the TRUTH have erred, saying that the resurrection is past already; and overthrow the faith of some. Nevertheless the foundation of God standeth sure, having this seal, The Lord knoweth them that are his. And, Let every one that nameth the name of Christ depart from iniquity. In meekness instructing those that oppose themselves; if God peradventure will give them repentance to the acknowledging of the TRUTH.
—2 Tim. 2. 18, 19, 25.

Ever learning, and never able to come to the knowledge of the TRUTH. —2 Tim. 3. 7.

Paul, a servant of God, and an apostle of Jesus Christ, according to the faith of God's elect, and the acknowledging of the TRUTH which is after godliness; in hope of eternal LIFE, which God, that cannot lie, promised before the world began. Not giving heed to Jewish fables, and commandments of men, that turn from the TRUTH. —Tit. 1. 1, 2, 14.

Every good gift and every perfect gift is from above, and cometh down from the Father of lights, with whom is no variableness, neither shadow of turning. Of his own will begat he us with the word of TRUTH, that we should be a kind of first-fruits of his creatures. —Jas. 1. 17, 18.

But if ye have bitter envying and strife in your hearts, glory not, and lie not against the TRUTH. —Jas. 3. 14.

Brethren, if any of you do err from the TRUTH, and one convert him; let him know, that he which converteth the sinner from the error of his WAY shall save a soul from death, and shall hide a multitude of sins.
—Jas. 5. 19, 20.

Seeing ye have purified yourselves in obeying the TRUTH through the Spirit unto unfeigned love of the brethren, see that ye love one another with a pure heart fervently: being born again, not of corruptible seed, but of incorruptible, by the word of God, which liveth and abideth forever. But the word of the Lord endureth forever. —1 Pet. 1. 22, 23, 25.

Wherefore I will not be negligent to put you always in remembrance of these things, though ye know them, and be established in the present TRUTH. —2 Pet. 1. 12.

And many shall follow their pernicious WAYS; by reason of whom the WAY of TRUTH shall be evil spoken of. —2 Pet. 2. 2.

That which we have seen and heard declare we unto you, that ye also may have fellowship with us: and truly our fellowship is with the Father, and with his Son Jesus Christ. This then is the message which we have heard of him, and declare unto you, that God is light, and in him is no darkness at all. If we say that we have fellowship with him, and walk in darkness, we lie, and do not the TRUTH: but if we walk in the light, as he is in the light, we have fellowship one with another, and the blood of Jesus Christ his Son cleanseth us from all sin. If we say that we have no sin, we deceive ourselves, and the TRUTH is not in us. If we confess our sins, he is faithful and just to forgive us our sins, and to cleanse us from all unrighteousness. —1 John 1. 3, 5-9.

He that saith, I know him, and keepeth not his commandments, is a liar, and the TRUTH is not in him. I have not written unto you because ye know not the TRUTH, but because ye know it, and that no lie is of the TRUTH. But the anointing which ye have received of him abideth in you, and ye need not that any man teach you: but as the same anointing teacheth you of all things, and is TRUTH, and is no lie, and even as it hath taught you, ye shall abide in him. —1 John 2. 4, 21, 27.

My little children, let us not love in word, neither in tongue; but in deed and in TRUTH. And hereby we know that we are of the TRUTH, and shall assure our hearts before him. —1 John 3. 18, 19.

He that knoweth God heareth us; he that is not of God heareth not us. Hereby know we the spirit of TRUTH, and the spirit of error. —1 John 4. 6.

This is he that came by water and blood, even Jesus Christ; not by water only, but by water and blood. And it is the Spirit that beareth witness, because the Spirit is TRUTH.
—1 John 5. 6.

Unto the elect lady and her children, whom I love in the TRUTH; and not I only, but also all they that have known the TRUTH; for the TRUTH'S sake, which dwelleth in us, and shall be with us forever. Grace be with you, mercy, and peace, from God the Father, and from the Lord Jesus Christ, the Son of the Father, in TRUTH and love. I rejoiced greatly that I found of thy children walking in TRUTH, as we have received a commandment from the Father. —2 John 1-4.

Unto the well beloved Gaius, whom I love in the TRUTH. Beloved, I wish above all things that thou mayest prosper and be in health, even as thy soul prospereth. For I rejoiced greatly, when the brethren came and testified of the TRUTH that is in thee, even as thou walkest in the TRUTH. I have no greater joy than to hear that my children walk in TRUTH. We therefore ought to receive such, that we might be fellow-helpers to the TRUTH. He that doeth good is of God: but he that doeth evil hath not seen God. (Jesus said at the beginning, the pure in heart shall see God.) Demetrius hath good report of all men, and of the TRUTH itself: yea, and we also bear record; and ye know that our record is TRUE. Greet the friends by name.
—3 John 1-4, 8, 11, 12, 14.

Jesus saith, I am the WAY, the TRUTH, and the LIFE: no man cometh unto the Father, but by me. —John 14. 6.

"Were the whole realm of nature mine,
  That were an offering far too small;
Love so amazing, so divine,
  Demands my LIFE, my soul, my all."

"Just as I am, young, strong, and free,
To be the best that I can be
For TRUTH and Righteousness and Thee,
  Lord of my LIFE, I come."

PROLUSION.

DEFINITION OF

By NOAH WEBSTER, LL.D.

ONE. That state of an animal or plant in which its organs are capable of performing their functions; animate existence; vitality; as, the LIFE of a tree, or a horse.

2. The time during which the human soul and body are united; the period between birth and death; the present state of existence; sometimes the perpetual existence of the soul in the present and future state.

She shows a body rather than a LIFE.—SHAK.

3. External manifestation of LIFE; conduct; deportment; as, to teach children to lead good LIVES.

4. A person or thing which imparts or excites spirit, vigor, or enjoyment; as, he was the LIFE of the company, or of the enterprise.

5. Animation; spirit; vivacity; briskness; vigor; energy.

They have no notion of LIFE and fire in fancy and words.—FELTON.

6. The living form; real person or state;—in opposition to a copy; as, a picture is taken from the LIFE; a description from the LIFE.

7. A person; a living being, usually or always a human being; as, how many LIVES were sacrificed during the Revolution.

8. The system of animal nature; animals in general, or considered collectively.

Full nature swarms with LIFE.—THOMSON.

9. Blood, as the supposed vehicle of animation.

The warm LIFE came issuing through the wound.—POPE.

10. Narrative of a past LIFE; history of the events of LIFE; as, Johnson wrote the LIFE of Milton, and the LIVES of other poets.

11. The attainment or experience of enjoyment in the right use of the powers; especially, happiness in the favor of God; eternal LIFE; heavenly felicity, in distinction from eternal death.

12. Position in society; rank, as determined by manner of LIVING; social state; as, high LIFE; low LIFE.

13. Common occurrences; as, related to the existence of human beings; course of things; human affairs.

> But to know
> That which before us lies in daily LIFE
> Is the prime wisdom.—MILTON.

14. That which is dear as one's existence; a darling; —often used as a term of endearment.

LIVE. The state of being alive.

LIFE. To have LIFE; to be animated; to possess capacity for the vital functions.

Dost thou love LIFE? Then do not squander time, for that is the stuff LIFE is made of.—FRANKLIN.

The truest end of LIFE is to know the LIFE that never ends.—WILLIAM PENN.

DEFINITION OF
SHIELD.

By NOAH WEBSTER, LL.D.

ONE. A broad piece of defensive armor, carried on the arm; a buckler;—formerly used in war for the protection of the body.

Now put your SHIELDS before your hearts and fight,
With hearts more proof than SHIELDS.—SHAK.

2. Any thing which protects or defends; defense; shelter; protection.

My council is my SHIELD.—SHAK.

SHIELD. To cover as with a SHIELD; to cover from danger; to defend; to protect; to secure from assault or injury.

SHIELD. To save LIFE, as a LIFE preserver.

The Lord is my strength and my SHIELD.—PSA. 28. 7.

  Safe as yon angelic bands;
  Safe as Gabriel where he stands;
  Safe as if around thy brow
  Wreathed the crown of glory now,
  And thy feet already trod
  The celestial mount of God.
     —LUCY A. BENNET.

In the WAY of righteousness is LIFE.
—Prov. 12. 28.

He layeth up sound wisdom for the righteous: he is a buckler to them that walk uprightly. —Prov. 2. 7.

Every word of God is pure: he is a SHIELD unto them that put their trust in him. —Prov. 30. 5.

Behold, O God our SHIELD, and look upon the face of thine anointed. —Psa. 84. 9.

Our soul waited for the Lord: he is our help and our SHIELD. —Psa. 33. 20.

The Lord is my rock, and my fortress, and my deliverer; the God of my rock; in him will I trust: he is my SHIELD, and the horn of my salvation, my high tower, and my refuge, my saviour. —2 Sam. 22. 2, 3.

The princes of the people are gathered together, even the people of the God of Abraham: for the SHIELDS of the earth belong unto God: he is greatly exalted. —Psa. 47. 9.

And he numbered them from twenty years old and above, and found them three hundred thousand choice men, able to go forth to war, that could handle spear and SHIELD.

—2 Chron. 25. 5.

The SHIELD of his mighty men is made red, the valiant men are in scarlet: the chariots shall be with flaming torches in the day of his preparation, and the fir-trees shall be terribly shaken. The chariots shall rage in the streets, they shall justle one against another in the broad WAYS: they shall seem like torches, they shall run like the lightnings.

—Nahum 2. 3, 4.

Thy light and TRUTH forth sending
  From thy own radiant side,
  Be thou our guard and guide;
On thee alone depending,
  No darkness can affright;
  Thy SHIELD of TRUTH and light,
  Clear flashing thro' the night,
Is all defending.   —F. R. Havergal.

LIFE.

FEAR not, Abram: I am thy SHIELD, and thy exceeding great reward.
—Gen. 15. 1.

HIS **TRUTH** SHALL BE THY **SHIELD** AND **BUCKLER.**
—Psa. 91. 4.

Stand therefore, having your loins girt about with TRUTH, and having on the breastplate of righteousness. —Eph. 6. 14.

Above all, taking the SHIELD of faith, wherewith ye shall be able to quench all the fiery darts of the wicked. —Eph. 6. 16.

And thine ears shall hear a word behind thee, saying, This is the WAY, walk ye in it.
—Isaiah.

Thou wilt show me the path of LIFE.
The paths of the Lord are mercy and TRUTH. —David.

"The WAY the holy prophets went,
The road that leads from banishment,
The KING'S HIGHWAY of HOLINESS,
I'll go, for all his paths are peace."

The PATH of the just is as the shining LIGHT, that shineth more and more unto the perfect day. —Solomon.

For with thee is the fountain of LIFE.
—David.

Old Testament.

PREFATORY BY MOSES.

In the BEGINNING—GOD created the heaven and the earth. . . . And the SPIRIT of GOD moved upon the face of the waters.

And GOD said, Let there be light. . . . And GOD saw the light, that it was GOOD. . . .

And GOD called the light Day. . . .

And GOD said, Let there be a firmament in the midst of the waters. . . .

And GOD made the firmament, and divided the waters which were under the firmament from the waters which were above the firmament. . . . And GOD called the firmament Heaven.

And GOD said, Let the waters under the heaven be gathered together unto one place, and let the dry land appear. . . .

And GOD called the dry land Earth; and the gathering together of the waters called the Seas: and GOD saw that it was GOOD.

And GOD said, Let the earth bring forth

grass, the herb yielding seed, and the fruit-tree yielding fruit after his kind, whose seed is in itself, upon the earth: . . . and GOD saw that it was GOOD.

And GOD said, Let there be lights in the firmament of the heaven to divide the day from the night; and let them be for signs, and for seasons, and for days, and years:

And let them be for lights in the firmament of the heaven to give light upon the earth. . . .

And GOD made two great lights; the greater light to rule the day, and the lesser light to rule the night: he made the stars also.

And GOD set them in the firmament of the heaven to give light upon the earth: . . . and GOD saw that it was GOOD.

And GOD said, Let the waters bring forth abundantly the moving creature that hath LIFE, and fowl that may fly above the earth in the open firmament of heaven.

And GOD created great whales, and every living creature that moveth, which the waters brought forth abundantly, after their kind, and every winged fowl after his kind: and GOD saw that it was GOOD.

And GOD blessed them, saying, Be fruitful and multiply. . . .

And GOD said, Let the earth bring forth the LIVING creature after his kind. . . .

And GOD made the beast of the earth after his kind, and cattle after their kind, and every thing . . . after his kind: and GOD saw that it was GOOD.

And GOD said, Let us make man in our image, after our likeness: and let them have dominion. . . .

So GOD created man in his own image, in the image of GOD created he him; male and female created he them.

And GOD blessed them, and GOD said unto them, Be fruitful, and multiply, and replenish the earth, and subdue it: and have dominion over the fish of the sea, and over the fowl of the air, and over every LIVING thing that moveth upon the earth.

And GOD said, Behold, I have given you

every herb bearing seed, which is upon the face of all the earth, and every tree, in the which is the fruit of a tree yielding seed; to you it shall be for meat [food].

And to every beast of the earth, and to every fowl of the air, and to every thing that creepeth upon the earth, wherein there is LIFE, I have given every green herb for meat. . . .

And GOD saw every thing that he had made, and, behold, it was VERY GOOD.

And GOD blessed the seventh day, and sanctified it. . . .

These are the generations of the heavens and of the earth when they were created. . . .
—Gen. 2. 3. 4.

And the Lord God formed man of the dust of the ground, and breathed into his nostrils the breath of LIFE; and man became a living soul. And the Lord God planted a garden eastward in Eden; and there he put the man whom he had formed. And out of the ground made the Lord God to grow every tree that is pleasant to the sight, and good for food; the tree of LIFE also in the midst of the garden. —Gen. 2. 7-9.

And the Lord said unto Noah, Come thou and all thy house into the ark; for thee have I seen righteous before me in this generation. In the six hundredth year of Noah's LIFE, in the second month, the seventeenth day of the month, the same day were all the fountains of the great deep broken up, and the windows of heaven were opened. And they went in unto Noah into the ark, two and two of all flesh, wherein is the breath of LIFE, . . . as God had commanded. . . . All in whose nostrils was the breath of LIFE. —Gen. 7. 1, 11, 15, 16, 22.

And God remembered Noah, and every LIVING thing, and all the cattle that was with him in the ark. And God spake unto Noah, saying, Go forth of the ark. . . . Bring forth with thee every LIVING thing that is with thee. —Gen. 8. 1, 15-17.

And God blessed Noah and his sons, and said unto them, Be fruitful, and multiply, and replenish the earth. And the fear of you and the dread of you shall be upon every beast of the earth, . . . into your hand are they delivered. Every moving thing that LIVETH shall be meat for you; even as the green herb have I given you all things. But flesh with the LIFE thereof, which is the blood thereof, shall ye not eat. And surely your blood of your LIVES will I require: at the hand of every beast will I require it, and at the hand of man; at the hand of every man's brother will I require the LIFE of man. . . . For in the image of God made he man. . . . And I will establish my covenant with you, . . . and with every LIVING creature. . . . This is the token of the covenant which I make between me and you, and every LIVING creature that is with you, for perpetual generations: I do set my bow in the cloud, and it shall be for a token of a covenant between me and the earth. And it shall come to pass, when I bring a cloud over the earth, that the bow shall be seen in the cloud: and I will remember my covenant, which is between me and you and every LIVING creature of all flesh; and the waters shall no more become a flood to destroy all flesh. And the bow shall be in the cloud; and I will look upon it, that I may remember the everlasting covenant between God and every LIVING creature of all flesh that is upon the earth. And God said unto Noah, This is the token of the covenant, which I have established between me and all flesh that is upon the earth. . . . And Noah lived [earth life] . . . nine hundred and fifty years. —Gen. 9. 1-17, 28, 29.

Is any thing too hard for the Lord? At the time appointed I will return unto thee, according to the time of LIFE, and Sarah shall have a son. —Gen. 18. 14.

And Lot said unto them, . . . Behold now, thy servant hath found grace in thy sight, and thou hast magnified thy mercy, which thou hast showed unto me in saving my LIFE.
—Gen. 19. 18, 19.

And Sarah was a hundred and seven and twenty years old: these were the years of the LIFE of Sarah. —Gen. 23. 1.

And Rebekah said to Isaac, I am weary of my LIFE because of the daughters of Heth: if Jacob take a wife of the daughters of Heth, such as these which are of the daughters of the land, what good shall my LIFE do me?
—Gen. 27. 46.

And Jacob called the name of the place Peniel: for I have seen God face to face, and my LIFE is preserved. —Gen. 32. 30.

Now therefore when I come to thy servant my father, and the lad be not with us; seeing that his LIFE is bound up in the lad's LIFE.
—Gen. 44. 30.

Now therefore be not grieved, nor angry with yourselves, that ye sold me hither; for God did send me before you to preserve LIFE. And God sent me before you to preserve you a posterity in the earth, and to save your LIVES by a great deliverance.
—Gen. 45. 5, 7.

And Jacob said unto Pharaoh, The days of the years of my pilgrimage are a hundred and thirty years: few and evil have the days of the years of my LIFE been, and have not attained unto the days of the years of the LIFE of my fathers in the days of their pilgrimage.
—Gen. 47. 9.

Joseph said unto them, Fear not: for am I in the place of God? But as for you, ye thought evil against me; but God meant it unto good, to bring to pass, as it is this day, to save much people ALIVE. —Gen. 50. 19, 20.

And Joseph dwelt in Egypt, he, and his father's house: and Joseph LIVED a hundred and ten years. —Gen. 50. 22.

And God said unto Moses, . . . Thus shalt thou say unto the children of Israel, I AM hath sent me unto you. —Exod. 3. 14.

Go, return into Egypt: for all the men are dead which sought thy LIFE. —Exod. 4. 19.

And he said, My presence shall go with thee. —Exod. 33. 14.

Ye shall therefore keep my statutes, and my judgments: which if a man do, he shall LIVE in them. —Lev. 18. 5.

And the Lord said, . . . As truly as I LIVE, all the earth shall be filled with the glory of the Lord. —Num. 14. 20, 21.

And the Lord said unto Moses, Make thee a fiery serpent, and set it upon a pole: and it shall come to pass, that every one that is bitten, when he looketh upon it, shall LIVE.
—Num. 21. 8.

All the commandments which I command thee this day shall ye observe to do, that ye may LIVE. —Deut. 8. 1.

That thou mayest remember the day when thou camest forth out of the land of Egypt all the days of thy LIFE. —Deut. 16. 3.

He shall write him a copy of this law in a book: . . . and he shall read therein all the days of his LIFE; that he may learn to fear the Lord his God, to keep all the words of this law. —Deut. 17. 18, 19.

To love the Lord thy God with all thine heart, and with all thy soul, that thou mayest LIVE. . . . See, I have set before thee this day LIFE and GOOD, . . . cleave unto him: for he is thy LIFE. —Deut. 30. 6, 15, 20.

The Lord shall judge his people. For I lift up my hand to heaven, and say, I LIVE forever.
—Deut. 32. 36, 40.

The eternal God is thy refuge, and underneath are the everlasting arms. —Deut. 33. 27.

There shall not any man be able to stand before thee all the days of thy LIFE: as I was with Moses, so I will be with thee: I will not fail thee, nor forsake thee. —Josh. 1. 5.

And Joshua said, Hereby ye shall know that the LIVING God is among you. —Josh. 3. 10.

And they feared him, as they feared Moses, all the days of his LIFE. —Josh. 4. 14.

And he shall be unto thee a restorer of thy LIFE, and a nourisher of thine old age.
—Ruth 4. 15.

And David said unto Saul, Who am I? and what is my LIFE, or my father's family in

Israel, that I should be son-in-law to the king? —1 Sam. 18. 18.

For he did put his LIFE in his hand, . . . and the Lord wrought a great salvation for all Israel. —1 Sam. 19. 5.

Abide thou with me, fear not: for he that seeketh my LIFE seeketh thy LIFE: but with me thou shalt be in safeguard.
—1 Sam. 22. 23.

A man is risen to pursue thee, and to seek thy soul: but the soul of my lord shall be bound in the bundle of LIFE with the Lord thy God. —1 Sam. 25. 29.

As the Lord liveth, . . . surely in what place my lord the king shall be, whether in death or LIFE, even there also will thy servant be.
—2 Sam. 15. 21.

The Lord LIVETH; and blessed be my rock; and exalted be the God of the rock of my salvation. —2 Sam. 22. 47.

Nathan spake unto Bath-sheba the mother of Solomon, saying, . . . Let me, I pray thee, give thee counsel, that thou mayest save thine own LIFE, and the LIFE of thy son Solomon. —1 Kings 1. 11, 12.

And Solomon said, . . . Give therefore thy servant an understanding heart, . . . to discern between good and bad: . . . and the speech pleased the Lord. . . . And God said unto him, Because thou hast asked this thing, and hast not asked for thyself long LIFE; neither hast asked riches for thyself, nor hast asked the LIFE of thine enemies; but hast asked for thyself understanding; . . . behold, I have done according to thy word: . . . if thou wilt walk in my WAYS. —1 Kings 3. 6-14.

And said unto him, O man of God, I pray thee, let my LIFE, and the LIFE of these fifty thy servants, be precious in thy sight.
—2 Kings 1. 13.

And it came to pass, as he was telling the king how he had restored a dead body to LIFE, that, behold, the woman, whose son he had restored to LIFE, cried to the king for her house and for her land. And Gehazi said,

My lord, O king, this is the woman, and this is her son, whom Elisha restored to LIFE.

—2 Kings 8. 5.

I sent messengers unto them, saying, I am doing a great work, so that I cannot come down: why should the work cease, whilst I leave it, and come down to you? And I said, Should such a man as I flee? and who is there, that, being as I am, would go into the temple to save his LIFE. —Neh. 6, 3, 11.

Then Esther the queen answered and said, If I have found favor in thy sight, O king, and if it please the king, let my LIFE be given me at my petition, and my people at my request.

—Esth. 7. 3.

Wherefore is light given to him that is in misery, and LIFE unto the bitter in soul.

—Job 3. 20.

Thou hast granted me LIFE and favor, and thy visitation hath preserved my SPIRIT.

—Job 10. 12.

The SPIRIT of God hath made me, and the breath of the Almighty hath given me LIFE.

—Job 33. 4.

BOOK OF PSALMS.

He asked LIFE of thee, and thou gavest it him, even length of days for ever and ever.

The meek shall eat and be satisfied: they shall praise the Lord that seek him: your heart shall LIVE forever.

Surely goodness and mercy shall follow me all the days of my LIFE.

One thing have I desired of the Lord, that will I seek after; that I may dwell in the house of the Lord all the days of my LIFE, and behold the beauty of the Lord, and to inquire in his temple.

What man is he that desireth LIFE, and loveth many days, that he may see good?

My soul thirsteth for God, for the living God: when shall I come and appear before God? Yet the Lord will command his loving-kindness in the daytime, and in the night his song shall be with me, and my prayer unto the God of my LIFE.

That he should still LIVE forever, and not see corruption.

Hear my voice, O God, in my prayer: preserve my LIFE from fear of the enemy.

And he shall LIVE, and to him shall be given of the gold of Sheba: prayer also shall be made for him continually.

Who redeemeth thy LIFE from destruction; who crowneth thee with loving-kindness and tender mercies.

I will sing unto the Lord as long as I LIVE: I will sing praise to my God while I have my being.

I will walk before the Lord in the land of the LIVING.

That I may LIVE, and keep thy word. That I may LIVE: for thy law is my delight. Uphold me according unto thy word, that I may LIVE: and let me not be ashamed of my hope. Let my soul LIVE, and it shall praise thee.

The Lord shall bless thee out of Zion: and thou shalt see the good of Jerusalem all the days of thy LIFE.

For there the Lord commanded the blessing, even LIFE for evermore.

PREFATORY BY SOLOMON.

My son, forget not my law; but let thine heart keep my commandments: for length of days, and long LIFE, and peace, shall they add to thee. Let not mercy and TRUTH forsake thee: bind them about thy neck; write them upon the table of thine heart. . . . Happy is the man that findeth wisdom, and the man that getteth understanding: for the merchandise of it is better than the merchandise of silver, and the gain thereof than fine gold. She is more precious than rubies: and all the things thou canst desire are not to be compared unto her. Length of days is in her right hand; and in her left hand riches and honor. Her WAYS are WAYS of pleasantness, and all her paths are peace. She is a tree of LIFE to them that lay hold upon her: and happy is every one that retaineth her. . . . So shall they be LIFE unto thy soul, and grace to thy neck.

Hear ye, children, . . . forsake ye not my law. . . . Keep my commandments and LIVE,

... and the years of thy LIFE shall be many.
... Take fast hold of instruction; ... for she is thy LIFE. ... For they are LIFE unto those that find them, and health to all their flesh.

Keep thy heart with all diligence; for out of it are the issues of LIFE.

Keep my commandments, and LIVE; and my law as the apple of thine eye.

For whoso findeth me findeth LIFE, and shall obtain favor of the Lord.

For by me thy days shall be multiplied, and the years of thy LIFE shall be increased.

The mouth of a righteous man is a well of LIFE.

The fruit of the righteous is a tree of LIFE; and he that winneth souls is wise.

The WAY of righteousness is LIFE; and in the pathway thereof there is no death.

He that keepeth his mouth keepeth his LIFE.

Hope deferred maketh the heart sick: but when the desire cometh, it is a tree of LIFE.

The law of the wise is a fountain of LIFE.

The fear of the Lord is a fountain of LIFE. A sound heart is the LIFE of the flesh.

A wholesome tongue is a tree of LIFE. The WAY of LIFE is above to the wise, that he may depart from hell beneath. The ear that heareth the reproof of LIFE abideth among the wise.

In the light of the king's countenance is LIFE; and his favor is as a cloud of the latter rain.

Death and LIFE are in the power of the tongue.

The fear of the Lord tendeth to LIFE: and he that hath it shall abide satisfied; he shall not be visited with evil.

He that followeth after righteousness and mercy findeth LIFE, righteousness, and honor.

By humility and the fear of the Lord are riches, and honor, and LIFE.

She will do him good and not evil all the days of her LIFE.

He hath made every thing beautiful in his time: also he hath set the world in their heart, so that no man can find out the work that God maketh from the beginning to the end. . . . There is no good in them, but for a man to rejoice, and to do good in his LIFE.

—Eccl. 3. 11, 12.

For wisdom is a defense, and money is a defense: but the excellency of knowledge is, that wisdom giveth LIFE. —Eccl. 7. 12.

The Lord was ready to save me: therefore we will sing my songs to the stringed instruments all the days of our LIFE in the house of the Lord. —Isa. 38. 20.

The Lord is the true God, he is the LIVING God, and an everlasting King. —Jer. 10. 10.

If the wicked restore the pledge, give again that he had robbed, walk in the statutes of LIFE, without committing iniquity; he shall surely LIVE. —Ezek. 33. 15.

I make a decree, That in every dominion of my kingdom men tremble and fear before the

God of Daniel: for he is the LIVING God, and steadfast forever. —Dan. 6. 26.

And many of them that sleep in the dust of the earth shall awake, some to everlasting LIFE, and some to shame and everlasting contempt. And they that be wise shall shine as the brightness of the firmament; and they that turn many to RIGHTEOUSNESS, as the stars for ever and ever. —Dan. 12. 2, 3.

Thus saith the Lord unto the house of Israel, Seek ye me, and ye shall LIVE.
—Amos 5. 4.

Hast thou brought up my LIFE from corruption, O Lord my God. —Jon. 2. 6.

Your fathers, where are they? and the prophets, do they LIVE forever? —Zech. 1. 5.

My covenant was with him of LIFE and peace. —Mal. 2. 5.

And the KEY of the house of David will I lay upon his shoulders. —Isaiah.

Arise, shine; for thy LIGHT is come, and the glory of the Lord is risen upon thee. —Isaiah

The COMMANDMENT is a lamp; and the law is light; and reproofs of instructions are the WAY of LIFE. —Solomon.

To such as keep his COVENANT. —David.

This is my COVENANT with them, saith the Lord: My SPIRIT that is upon thee, and my words that I have put in thy mouth, shall not depart out of thy mouth, nor out of the mouth of thy seed's seed, saith the Lord, from henceforth and forever. —Isaiah.

My covenant is with him of LIFE and PEACE. —Malachi.

His kingdom is an everlasting kingdom.
—Daniel.

Jesus shall reign where'er the sun
Does his successive journeys run ;
His KINGDOM spread from shore to shore,
Till moons shall wax and wane no more.
—Watts.

JESUS SAITH:

Think not that I am come to destroy the LAW, or the prophets: I am not come to destroy, but to fulfill. . . . WHOSOEVER therefore shall break one of these least commandments, and shall TEACH men so, he shall be called the least in the KINGDOM of HEAVEN: but WHOSOEVER shall DO and TEACH THEM, the same shall be called great in the KINGDOM of HEAVEN.

For I say unto you, That EXCEPT your righteousness shall exceed the righteousness of the scribes and Pharisees, ye shall in no case enter into the KINGDOM of HEAVEN.

EXCEPT ye be born again, ye cannot enter the KINGDOM OF HEAVEN. And except ye be converted, and become as little children, ye cannot ENTER the KINGDOM of HEAVEN.

For the KINGDOM of HEAVEN is within you, and shall be in you a well of water springing up unto everlasting LIFE.

Fear not, little flock, for it is your FA-

THER'S GOOD pleasure to give you THE KINGDOM.

AND HE SHALL SAY.

Come, ye blessed of my Father, inherit the KINGDOM prepared for you from the foundation of the world.

Of his KINGDOM there shall be no end.
—Luke.

———

In the light of the KING'S countenance is LIFE.

"We are watching, we are waiting,
   For the beauteous King of day;
For the Chiefest of ten thousand,
   For the LIFE, the TRUTH, the WAY."

———

Lift up your heads, O ye gates; even lift them up, ye everlasting DOORS; and the KING of GLORY shall come in. Who is this KING of GLORY? —David.

And the posts of the DOOR moved at the voice of him that cried. —Isaiah.

Behold, I have set before you an OPEN DOOR, and no man can shut it.

After this I looked, and, behold, a DOOR was opened in HEAVEN. —Revelation of John.

Jesus saith, I AM the DOOR, by me if any man enter in, he shall be saved, and shall go in and out, and find pasture.

Then said Jesus unto them again, Verily, verily, I say unto you, I AM the DOOR of the sheep.

I AM the GOOD SHEPHERD: the GOOD SHEPHERD giveth his LIFE for the sheep.

He that followeth me shall not walk in darkness, but shall have the LIGHT of LIFE.

And he shall bring forth the HEADSTONE thereof with shoutings, crying, GRACE, GRACE unto it. —Zechariah.

As it is written, The first man, Adam, was made a LIVING SOUL; the last Adam was made a quickening SPIRIT.

As in Adam all die, even so in Christ shall all be made ALIVE. —Paul.

Jesus said, . . . I AM come that they might have LIFE, and that they might have it more ABUNDANTLY.

And he breathed upon them and said, Receive ye the HOLY GUEST.

It is thy LIFE alone, alone thy LIFE,
      That saveth me;
And for that LIFE of thine, that saving LIFE,
      I come to thee. —Bonar.

    Amen, so let it be!
LIFE from the dead is in that word,
    'Tis IMMORTALITY. —Montgomery.

New Testament.

PREFATORY BY MATTHEW.

The book of the generations of Jesus Christ, the son of David, the son of Abraham. . . .

Now the birth of Jesus Christ was on this wise: When as his mother Mary was espoused to Joseph, before they came together, she was found with child of the Holy GUEST. . . . The angel of the Lord appeared unto him in a dream, saying, Joseph, . . . that which is conceived in her is of the Holy GUEST. And she shall bring forth a son, and thou shalt call his name JESUS: for he shall save his people from their sins. . . . Which was spoken of the Lord by the prophet. . . . They shall call his name Emmanuel, . . . God with us. Then Joseph being raised from sleep did as the ANGEL of the Lord had bidden him. . . . and called his NAME JESUS.

JESUS was born in Bethlehem, . . . and behold there came wise men from the east to Jerusalem, saying, Where is he that is born KING? . . . we have seen his STAR in the east, . . . and, lo, the star, which they saw in the east, went before them, till it came and stood over where the young child was. When they saw the ☆, they rejoiced with exceeding great joy.

The ANGEL of the Lord appeareth to Joseph in a dream, saying, Arise, and take the young child and his mother, and flee into Egypt, and be thou there until I bring thee word : . . . which was spoken by the prophet, saying, Out of Egypt have I called my son. . . . An ANGEL of the Lord appeareth in a dream to Joseph in Egypt, saying, Arise, and take the young child and his mother, and go into the land of Israel: for they are dead which sought the young child's LIFE. . . . And they dwelt in a city called Nazareth : . . . which was spoken by the prophets, He shall be called a Nazarene. . . . That it might be fulfilled which was spoken by Esaias the prophet. . . . The people which sat in darkness saw great LIGHT ; and to them which sat in the region and shadow of death light is sprung up.

PREFATORY TO THE MINISTRY OF JESUS.

Then cometh Jesus from Galilee to Jordan unto John, to be baptized of him. But John forbade him, saying, I have need to be baptized of thee, and comest thou to me? And Jesus answering said unto him, Suffer it to be so now: for thus it becometh us to fulfill all RIGHTEOUSNESS. . . . And JESUS, when he was baptized, went up straightWAY out of the water: and, lo, the heavens were opened unto him, and he saw the SPIRIT of GOD descending like a DOVE, and lighted upon him: and lo a voice from heaven, saying, This is my beloved Son, in whom I am well pleased.

> Come, Holy GUEST, our souls inspire,
> And lighten with celestial fire;
> Thou the anointing SPIRIT art,
> Who dost thy sevenfold gifts impart;
> Thy blessed unction from above
> Is comfort, LIFE, and flame of LOVE.
> Gregory the Great.

THE TEMPTATION.

Then was Jesus led up of the SPIRIT into the wilderness to be tempted of the devil. And when he had fasted forty days and forty nights, he was afterward a hungered. And when the tempter came to him, he said, If thou be the Son of God, command that these stones be made bread. But he answered and said, It is written, Man shall not live by bread alone, but by every WORD that proceedeth out of the mouth of God. Then the devil taketh him up into the holy city, and setteth him on a pinnacle of the temple, and saith unto him, If thou be the Son of God, cast thyself down: for it is written. . . . Jesus said unto him, It is written again, Thou shalt not tempt the Lord thy God. Again, the devil taketh him up into an exceeding high mountain, and showeth him all the kingdoms of the world, and the glory of them; and saith unto him, All these things will I give thee, if thou wilt fall down and worship me. Then saith Jesus unto him, Get thee hence, Satan: for it is written, Thou shalt worship the Lord thy God, and him only shalt thou serve. Then the devil leaveth him, and, behold, ANGELS came and ministered unto him.

From that time JESUS begun to preach, and to say, Repent: for the KINGDOM of HEAVEN is at hand, . . . TEACHING, . . . and preaching the gospel of the KINGDOM, and healing all manner of sickness and all manner of disease among the people. . . . And they brought unto him all sick people that were taken with divers diseases and torments, . . . and those which were lunatic, and those that had the palsy; and he healed them.

And seeing the multitudes, he went up into a mountain: and when he was set, his disciples came unto him: and he opened his mouth, and taught them, saying, Blessed are the poor in SPIRIT: for theirs is the KINGDOM OF HEAVEN.

Blessed are they which are persecuted for RIGHTEOUSNESS' sake: for theirs is the KINGDOM of HEAVEN.

Ye are the SALT of the earth.

Ye are the light of the world. A city that is set on a hill cannot be hid. Neither do men light a candle, and put it under a bushel, but on a candlestick; and it giveth LIGHT unto all that are in the house.

Let your LIGHT so SHINE before men, that they may see your GOOD works, and glorify your FATHER which is in heaven.

If thou bring thy gift to the ALTAR, and there rememberest that thy brother hath aught against thee; leave there thy gift before the ALTAR, and go thy WAY; first be reconciled to thy brother, and then come and offer thy gift.

But I say unto you, Love your enemies, . . . that ye may be the children of your FATHER which is in HEAVEN.

Take heed that ye do not your alms before men, to be seen of them: otherwise ye have no reward of your FATHER which is in Heaven.

After this manner therefore pray ye: Our 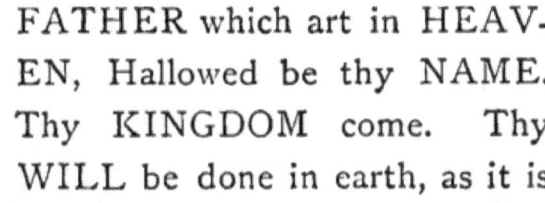 FATHER which art in HEAVEN, Hallowed be thy NAME. Thy KINGDOM come. Thy WILL be done in earth, as it is in HEAVEN. Give us this day our daily bread. And forgive us our debts, as we forgive our debtors. And [leave] us not in temptation, but deliver us from evil: For thine is the KINGDOM, and the power, and the glory, forever. Amen.

Let no man say when he is tempted, I am tempted of God: for God cannot be tempted with evil, neither tempteth he any man.—James.

The Lord knoweth how to deliver the godly out of temptation. —Peter.

God is faithful, who will not suffer you to be tempted above that ye are able: but will with the temptation also make a WAY to escape, that ye may be able to bear it.

For we have not a high-PRIEST which cannot be touch with the feeling of our infirmities; but was in all points tempted like as we are, yet without sin.

For in that he himself hath suffered being tempted, he is able to succor them that are tempted. —Paul.

The light of the body is the eye: if therefore thine be single, thy whole body shall b e full of LIGHT.

Therefore I say unto you, Take no thought for your LIFE. . . . Is not the LIFE more than meat, and the body than raiment? Behold the fowls of the air. . . . Your heavenly FATHER feedeth them. . . . Consider the lilies of the field. . . . But seek ye first the KINGDOM of GOD and his RIGHTEOUSNESS; and all these things shall be added unto you. Take therefore no thought for the morrow.

Judge not, that ye be not judged.

Ask, and it shall be given you.

Enter ye in at the strait gate. . . . Because strait is the gate, and narrow is the WAY, which leadeth unto LIFE.

Ye shall know them by their fruits. . . . Every GOOD tree bringeth forth GOOD fruit.

Not every one that saith unto me, Lord, Lord, shall enter into the KINGDOM of HEAVEN. . . . Therefore WHOSOEVER heareth these sayings of mine and doeth them, I will liken him unto a wise man, which built his house upon a ROCK. . . . And it came to pass, when Jesus had ended these sayings, the people were astonished at his doctrine: for he TAUGHT as one having authority, and not as the scribes.

For all the prophets and the law prophesied until John. And if ye will receive it, this is Elias which was for to come. He that hath ears to hear, let him hear.

And from the days of John the Baptist until now the KINGDOM of HEAVEN suffereth violence, and the violent taketh it by force.

And Jesus knew their thoughts, and said

unto them, Every kingdom divided against itself is brought to desolation. . . . But if I cast out devils by the SPIRIT of GOD, then the KINGDOM of GOD is come unto you.

But blessed are your eyes, for they see; and your ears, for they hear. For verily I say unto you, That many prophets and righteous men have desired to see those things which ye see, and have not seen them; and to hear those things which ye hear, and have not heard them.

When he was come down from the mountain, great multitudes followed him. And, behold, there came a leper and worshiped him, saying, Lord, if thou wilt, thou canst make me clean. And Jesus put forth his hand, and touched him, saying, I will; be thou CLEAN.

And I say unto you, That many shall come from the east and the west, and shall sit down with Abraham, and Isaac, and Jacob, in the KINGDOM of HEAVEN.

While he spake these things unto them, behold, there came a certain ruler, and worshiped him, saying, My daughter is even now dead: but come and lay thy hand upon her, and she shall LIVE. And Jesus arose, and followed him. . . . He went in, and took her by the hand, and the maid arose.

Jesus went about all the cities and villages, TEACHING . . . and PREACHING the GOSPEL of the KINGDOM, and healing every sickness and every disease among the people. . . . Then saith he unto his disciples, The harvest truly is plenteous, but the laborers are few; pray ye therefore the Lord of the harvest, that he will send forth laborers into his harvest. And when he had called unto him his twelve disciples, he gave them power against unclean spirits, to cast them out, and to heal all manner of sickness and all manner of disease. . . . These twelve Jesus sent forth, and commanded them, saying, Go. . . . And as ye go, preach, saying, The KINGDOM of HEAVEN is at hand. Heal the sick, cleanse the lepers, raise the dead, cast out devils: freely ye have received, freely give.

Behold, I send you forth as sheep in the midst of wolves: be ye therefore wise as serpents, and harmless as doves. . . . For it is not ye that speak, but the SPIRIT of your FATHER which speaketh in you.

He that findeth his LIFE shall lose it: and he that loseth his LIFE for my sake shall find it. —Matt. 10. 39.

And Jesus stretched forth his hand toward his disciples, and said, Behold my mother and my brethren! For whosoever shall do the will of my FATHER which is in HEAVEN, the same is my brother, and sister, and mother.
—Matt. 12. 49, 50.

And his disciples came and said unto him, Why speakest thou unto them in parables? He answered, . . . Because it is given unto you to know the mysteries of the KINGDOM of HEAVEN. . . . Hear ye therefore the parable of the sower.

Another parable put he forth unto them, saying, The KINGDOM of HEAVEN is likened unto a man which sowed GOOD seed in his field.

Another parable put he forth unto them, saying, The KINGDOM of HEAVEN is like a grain of mustard seed, which a man took, and sowed in his field.

Another parable spake he unto them; The KINGDOM of HEAVEN is like unto leaven, which a woman took, and hid in three measures of meal, till the whole was leavened.

Again, the KINGDOM of HEAVEN is like unto treasure hid in a field; the which when a man hath found, he hideth, and for joy thereof goeth and selleth all that he hath, and buyeth that field.

Again, the KINGDOM of HEAVEN is like unto a merchantman, seeking goodly pearls; who, when he had found one pearl of great price, went and sold all that he had, and bought it.

Again, the KINGDOM of HEAVEN is like a net, that was cast into the sea, and gathered of every kind: which, when it was full, they drew to shore, and set down, and gathered the GOOD into vessels, but cast the bad away.

Jesus saith unto them, Have ye understood all these things? They say unto him, Yea, Lord. Then said he unto them, Therefore every scribe which is instructed unto the KINGDOM of HEAVEN, is like unto a man that is a householder, which bringeth forth out of his treasure things new and old.

And he called the multitude, and said unto them, Hear, and understand.

And when the disciples saw him walking on the sea, they were troubled, saying, It is a spirit; and they cried out for fear. But straightway Jesus spake unto them, saying, Be of good cheer; it is I; be not afraid.

And he called the multitude, and said unto them, Hear, and understand: Not that which goeth into the mouth defileth a man; but that which cometh out of the mouth, this defileth a man.

Jesus . . . asked HIS DISCIPLES, saying, Whom do men say that I, the Son of man, am? . . . Simon Peter answered and said, Thou art the Christ, the Son of the LIVING GOD. And

Jesus answered and said, . . . Upon this ROCK I will build my CHURCH; and the gates of hell shall not prevail against it. And I will give unto thee [his disciples] the KEYS of the KINGDOM of HEAVEN.

He turned, and said unto Peter, Get thee behind me, Satan: thou art an offense unto me: for thou savorest not the things that be of God, but those that be of men. . . . For whosoever will save his LIFE shall lose it: and whosoever will lose his LIFE for my sake shall find it. . . . Verily I say unto you, There be some standing here, which shall not taste of death, till they see the Son of man coming in his KINGDOM.

At the same time came the disciples unto Jesus, saying, Who is the greatest in the KINGDOM of HEAVEN? . . . Whosoever therefore shall humble himself as this little child, the same is greatest in the KINGDOM of HEAVEN.

It is better for thee to enter into LIFE halt or maimed, rather than having two hands or two feet to be cast into everlasting fire. . . . It is better to enter into LIFE with one eye, rather than having two eyes to be cast into hell fire.

The Son of man is come to save that which was lost. . . . Even so it is not the will of your FATHER which is in HEAVEN, that one of these little ones should perish.

Therefore is the KINGDOM of HEAVEN likened unto a certain king, which would take account of his servants.

So likewise shall my HEAVENLY FATHER do also unto you, if ye from your hearts forgive not every one his brother their trespasses.

And he answered and said unto them, Have ye not read, That he which made them at the beginning made them male and female, and said, For this cause shall a man leave father and mother; . . . and they twain shall be one flesh? . . . But he said unto them, All men cannot receive this saying, save they to whom it is given, . . . for the kingdom of heaven's sake.

He that is able to receive it, let him receive it.

Then were there brought unto him little children, that he should put his hands on them, and pray: ... Jesus said, Suffer little children, and forbid them not, to come unto me: for of such is the KINGDOM of HEAVEN. And he laid his hands on them, and departed thence.

And behold, one came and said unto him, Good Master, what good thing shall I do, that I may have eternal LIFE? And he said unto him, Why callest thou me good? there is none good but one, that is, God: but if thou wilt enter into LIFE, keep the commandments. ... The young man saith unto him, All these things have I kept from my youth up: what lack I yet? Jesus said unto him, If thou wilt be perfect, go and sell that thou hast, and give to the poor, and thou shalt have treasure in heaven: and come and follow me.

Then said Jesus unto his disciples, Verily I say unto you, That a rich man shall hardly enter into the KINGDOM of HEAVEN. ...

But with God all things are possible. . . . And every one that hath forsaken houses, or brethren, or sisters, or father, or mother, or wife, or children, or lands, for my name's sake, shall receive a hundredfold, and shall inherit everlasting LIFE.

The KINGDOM of HEAVEN is like unto a man that is a householder, which went out early in the morning to hire laborers into his vineyard. And when he had agreed with the laborers for a penny a day, he sent them into his vineyard.

And Jesus going up to Jerusalem, . . . then came to him the mother of Zebedee's children. . . . And he said unto her, What wilt thou? She saith unto him, Grant that these my two sons may sit, the one on thy right hand, and the other on the left, in THY KINGDOM. But Jesus answered and said, Ye know not what ye ask. . . . To sit on my right hand, and on my left, is not mine to give, but it shall be given to them for whom it is prepared of my Father. . . . Even as the Son of man came not to be ministered unto, but to minister, and to give his LIFE a ransom for many.

And when they drew nigh unto Jerusalem, and were come to Bethphage, unto the mount of Olives, then Jesus sent two disciples, saying unto them, Go into the village over against you, and straightWAY ye shall find an ass tied, and a colt with her: loose them, and bring them unto me. . . . That it might be fulfilled which was spoken by the prophet, saying, Tell ye the daugter of Sion, Behold, thy KING cometh unto thee, meek, and sitting upon an ass, . . . the foal of an ass. . . . And the multitudes that went before, and that followed, cried, saying, Hosanna to the SON of DAVID: Blessed is he that cometh in the name of the Lord; Hosanna in the highest. . . . And when he was come into Jerusalem, . . . the multitude said, This is JESUS the prophet of Nazareth of Galilee.

And Jesus went into the temple of God. . . . And the blind and the lame came to him in the temple; and he healed them. . . . And the children crying in the temple, and saying, Hosanna to the Son of David.

And he left them, and went out of the city into Bethany; and he lodged there. Now in the morning, as he returned into the city, he hungered. And when he saw a fig-tree in the WAY, he came to it, and found nothing thereon, but leaves only. . . . Jesus answered and said, . . . If ye have faith, and doubt not, . . . all things WHATSOEVER ye shall ask in prayer, believing, ye shall receive.

And when he was come into the temple, the chief priests and the elders of the people came unto him as he was teaching, and said, By what authority doest thou these things? and who gave thee this authority? Jesus answered and said unto them, I also will ask you one thing, which if ye tell me, I in like wise will tell you by what authority I do these things. The baptism of John, whence was it? from heaven, or of men? And they reasoned with themselves, saying, If we shall say, From heaven. . . . And they answered Jesus, and said, We cannot tell. And he said unto them, Neither tell I you by what authority I do these things.

But what think ye? A certain man had two sons; and he came to the first, and said, Son, go work to-day in my vineyard. He answered and said, I will not; but afterward he repented, and went. And he came to the second, and said likewise. And he answered and said, I go, sir; and went not. Whether of them twain did the will of his father? They say unto him, The first. Jesus saith unto them, Verily I say unto you, That the publicans and the harlots go into the KINGDOM of GOD before you.

For John came unto you in the WAY of righteousness, and ye believed him not; but the publicans and the harlots believed him.

Hear another parable: There was a certain householder, which planted a vineyard, . . . and let it out to husbandmen. . . . And when the time of the fruit drew near, he sent his servants to the husbandmen, that they might receive the fruits of it. And the husbandmen

. . . beat one, and killed another, and stoned another. . . . But last of all he sent unto them his son, saying, They will reverence my son. . . . And they caught him, and cast him out of the vineyard, and slew him.

Jesus saith unto them, Did ye never read in the Scriptures, The stone which the builders rejected, the same is become the head of the corner: this is the Lord's doing, and is marvelous in our eyes? Therefore say I unto you, The KINGDOM of GOD shall be taken from you, and given to a nation bringing forth the fruits thereof.

And Jesus . . . spake unto them again by parables, and said, The KINGDOM of HEAVEN is like unto a certain king, which made a marriage for his son, and sent forth his servants to call those that were bidden to the wedding: and they would not come. . . . Then saith he to his servants, The wedding is ready, but they which were bidden were not worthy. Go ye therefore into the HIGHWAYS, and as many as ye shall find, bid to the marriage. . . . And the wedding was furnished with guests.

Then went the Pharisees, and took counsel, how they might entangle him in his talk. . . . But Jesus perceived their wickedness, . . . and said unto them, Ye do err, not knowing the SCRIPTURES, nor the power of God. For in the resurrection they neither marry, or are given in marriage, but are as the angels of GOD in HEAVEN. But as touching the resurrection of the dead, have ye not read that which was spoken unto you by God, saying, I am the God of Abraham, and the God of Isaac, and the God of Jacob? God is not the God of the dead, but of the LIVING. And when the multitude heard this, they were astonished at his doctrine.

But when the Pharisees had heard that he had put the Sadducees to silence, they were gathered together. Then one of them, which was a lawyer, asked him a question, tempting him, and saying, Master, which is the great commandment in the law? Jesus said unto him, Thou shalt LOVE the Lord thy God with all thy heart, and with all thy soul, and with all thy mind. This is the first and great commandment. And the second is like unto it, Thou shalt LOVE thy neighbor as thyself. On these two commandments hang all the law and the prophets.

But woe unto you, scribes and Pharisees, hypocrites! for ye shut up the KINGDOM of HEAVEN against men.

Wherefore, behold, I send unto you prophets, and wise men, and scribes: and some of them ye shall kill and crucify; and some of them shall ye scourge in your synagogues, and persecute them from city to city. . . . For I say unto you, Ye shall not see me henceforth, till ye shall say, Blessed is he that cometh in the NAME of the Lord.

And this gospel of the KINGDOM shall be preached in all the world for a witness unto all nations; and then shall the end come.

And then shall appear the sign of the Son of man . . . coming in the clouds of HEAVEN with power and great glory. And he shall send his angels with a great sound of a trumpet. See Psa. 103. 20–22.

Heaven and earth shall pass away, but my WORDS shall not pass away.

But of that day and hour knoweth no man, no, not the angels of heaven, but my Father only.

Watch therefore ; for ye know not what hour your Lord doth come.

Therefore be ye also ready. . . . Blessed is that servant, whom his lord when he cometh shall find so doing.

Then shall the KINGDOM of HEAVEN be likened unto ten virgins, which took their lamps, and went forth to meet the bridegroom. And five of them were wise, and five were foolish. They that were foolish took their lamps, and took no oil with them : but the wise took oil in their vessels with their lamps. . . . At midnight there was a cry made, Behold, the bridegroom cometh ; go ye out to meet him. Then all those virgins arose, and trimmed their lamps. And the foolish said unto the wise, Give us of your oil ; for our lamps are gone out. But the wise answered, saying, Not so ;

lest there be not enough for us and you: but go ye rather to them that sell, and buy for yourselves. And while they went to buy, the bridegroom came; and they that were ready, went in with him to the marriage: and the DOOR was shut.

For the kingdom of heaven is as a man traveling into a far country, who called his own servants, and delivered unto them his goods. And unto one he gave five talents, to another two, and to another one; to every man according to his several ability; and STRAIGHTWAY took his journey. . . . After a long time the lord of those servants cometh, and reckoneth with them.

When the SON of man shall come in his glory, and all the holy angels with him, then shall he sit upon the throne of his glory: and before him shall be gathered all nations: and he shall separate them one from another, as a shepherd divideth his sheep from the goats. . . . Then shall the KING say unto them on his right hand, Come, ye blessed of my

FATHER, inherit the KINGDOM prepared for you from the foundation of the world. . . . And the KING shall answer and say unto them, Verily I say unto you, Inasmuch as ye have done it unto one of the least of these my brethren, ye have done it unto me. . . . The righteous into LIFE ETERNAL.

And it came to pass, when Jesus had finished all these sayings, he said unto his disciples, Ye know that after two days is the feast of the passover, and the Son of man is betrayed to be crucified.

When Jesus was in Bethany, in the house of Simon the leper, there came unto him a woman having an alabaster box of very precious ointment, and poured it on his head, as he sat at meat. But when his disciples saw it, they had indignation, saying, To what purpose is this waste? For this ointment might have been sold for much, and given to the poor. When Jesus understood it, he said unto them, Why trouble ye the woman? for she hath wrought a GOOD work upon me. For ye have the poor always with you; but me ye have not always. For in that she hath poured this ointment on my body, she did it for my burial. Verily I say unto you, WHERESO-EVER this GOSPEL shall be preached in the whole world, there shall also this, that this woman hath done, be told for a MEMORIAL of her.

The Master saith, My time is at hand; I will keep the passover . . . with my disciples. Now when the even was come, he sat down with the twelve.

And as they were eating, Jesus took bread, and blessed it, and brake it, and gave it to the disciples, and said, Take, eat; this is my body. And he took the cup, and gave thanks, and gave it to them, saying, Drink ye all of it; for this is my blood of the NEW TESTAMENT, which is shed for many for the remission of sins. But I say unto you, I will not drink henceforth of this fruit of the vine, until that day when I drink it new with you in my FA-THER'S KINGDOM. And when they had sung a hymn, they went out into the mount of Olives.

Then cometh Jesus with them unto a place called Gethsemane, and saith unto the disciples, Sit ye here, while I go and pray yonder. . . . And he went a little further, and fell on his face, and prayed, saying, O my Father, if it be possible, let this cup pass from me: nevertheless, not as I will, but as thou wilt. . . . He went away again the second time, and prayed, saying, O my Father, if this cup may not pass away from me, except I drink it, thy will be done. . . . And he . . . went away again, and prayed the third time, saying the same words. Then cometh he to his disciples, and saith unto them, . . . Rise, let us be going: behold, he is at hand that doth betray me. . . . Now he that betrayed him gave a sign. . . . And forthwith he came to Jesus, . . . and kissed him. And Jesus said unto him, Friend, wherefore are thou come? . . . Thinkest thou that I cannot now pray to my Father, and he shall presently give me more than twelve legions of ANGELS? . . . In that same hour said Jesus to the multitudes, Are ye come out as against a thief with swords and staves for to take me? I sat daily with you teaching in the temple, and ye laid no hold on me.

And they . . . led him away to Caiaphas the high-priest. . . . The high-priest arose, and said unto him, Answerest thou nothing? . . . But Jesus held his peace. And the high-priest answered and said unto him, I adjure thee by the LIVING GOD, that thou tell us whether thou be THE CHRIST, the Son of God. Jesus saith unto him, Thou hast said: nevertheless I say unto you, Hereafter shall ye see the Son of man sitting on the right hand of power, and coming in the clouds of heaven.

When the morning was come, all the chief priests and elders of the people took counsel against Jesus to put him to death. . . . And Jesus stood before the governor: and the governor asked him, saying, Art thou the King of the Jews? And Jesus said unto him, Thou sayest. And when he was accused of the chief priests and elders, he answered nothing. Then said Pilate unto him, Hearest thou not how many things they witness against thee? . . . And he answered him never a word.

At that feast the governor was wont to release unto the people a prisoner, whom they would. . . . Pilate said unto them, Whom will ye that I release unto you? Barabbas, or Jesus which is called Christ? For he knew that for envy they had delivered him.

When he was set down on the judgment-seat, his wife sent unto him, saying, Have thou nothing to do with that just man: for I have suffered many things this day in a dream because of him.

When Pilate saw that he could prevail nothing, but that rather a tumult was made, he took water, and washed his hands before the multitude, saying, I am innocent of the blood of this just person: see ye to it.

And when they had platted a crown of thorns, they put it upon his head, and a reed in his right hand: . . . and led him away to crucify him. And as they came out, they found a man of Cyrene, Simon by name: him they compelled to bear his cross. . . . When they were come unto a place called Golgotha, . . . they gave him vinegar to drink mingled with gall: and when he had tasted thereof, he would not drink.

And they crucified him. . . . And set up over his head his accusation written. This is Jesus the King of the Jews. Then were there two thieves crucified with him.

Jesus, when he had cried again with a loud voice, yielded up the GUEST. And, behold, the vail of the temple was rent in twain from the top to the bottom; and the earth did quake, and the rocks rent.

And when Joseph had taken the body, he wrapped it in a clean linen cloth, and laid it in his own new tomb, which he had hewn out in the rock: and rolled a great stone to the door of the sepulcher, and departed. And there was Mary Magdalene, and the other Mary, sitting over against the sepulcher.

THE RESURRECTION.

As it began to dawn toward the first day of the week, came Mary Magdalene and the other Mary to see the sepulcher. And, behold, there was a great earthquake: for the ANGEL of the Lord descended from HEAVEN, and came and rolled back the stone from the DOOR, and sat upon it. His countenance was like lightning, and his raiment white as snow: and for fear of him the keepers did shake, and became as dead men. . . . And the graves were opened; and many bodies of the saints which slept arose, and came out of the graves after his resurrection, and went into the holy city, and appeared unto many. . . . And the ANGEL answered and said unto the women, Fear not ye: for I know that ye seek Jesus, which was crucified. He is not here: for he is RISEN, as he said. Come, see the place where the Lord lay. And go quickly, and tell his disciples that he is risen from the dead; and, behold, he goeth before you into Galilee; there shall ye see him: lo, I have told you. And they departed quickly from the sepulcher with fear and great joy; and did run to bring his disciples word.

And as they went to tell his disciples, behold, Jesus met them, saying, All hail! And they came and held him by the feet, and worshiped him. Then said Jesus unto them, Be not afraid: go tell my brethren that they go into Galilee, and there shall they see me.

Then the eleven disciples went away into Galilee, into a mountain where Jesus had appointed them. And when they saw him, they worshiped him: but some doubted. And Jesus came and spake unto them, saying, All POWER is given unto ME in HEAVEN and in EARTH.

Go ye therefore, and TEACH all nations, baptizing them in the NAME of the FATHER, and of the SON, and of the HOLY GUEST: TEACHING them to observe all things WHATSOEVER I have commanded you: and, lo, I AM with you alway, even unto the end of the world. Amen.

PREFATORY BY LUKE.

FORASMUCH as many have taken in hand to set forth in order a declaration of those things which are most surely believed among us, even as they delivered them unto us, which from the beginning were eye-witnesses, and ministers of the word; it seemed good to me also, having had perfect understanding of all things from the very first, to write unto thee in order, most excellent Theophilus, that thou mightest know the certainty of those things, wherein thou hast been instructed.

The angel Gabriel was sent from God unto a city of Galilee, named Nazareth, to a virgin espoused to a man whose name was Joseph, of the house of David; and the virgin's name was Mary. And the ANGEL came in unto her, and said, Hail, thou that art highly favored, the Lord is with thee: blessed art thou among women. And when she saw him, she was troubled at his saying. . . . And the ANGEL said unto her, Fear not, Mary: for thou hast found favor with God. And, behold, thou shalt conceive, . . . and bring forth a son, and shalt call his name JESUS. . . . And shall be called the Son of the Highest; . . . and of his KINGDOM there shall be no end.

Then said Mary unto the ANGEL, How shall this be? . . . And the ANGEL answered and said unto her, The HOLY GUEST shall come upon thee, and the POWER of the Highest shall overshadow thee: therefore also that holy thing which shall be born of thee shall be called the SON of GOD. . . . For with God nothing shall be impossible.

And Mary said, Behold the handmaid of the Lord; be it unto me according to THY WORD.

And Mary said, My SOUL doth magnify the Lord, and my SPIRIT hath rejoiced in GOD my SAVIOUR.

For he hath regarded the low estate of his handmaiden: for, behold, from henceforth all generations shall call me blessed. [Blessed motherhood.]

For HE that is mighty hath done to me great things; and holy is his NAME.

As HE spake to our fathers, to Abraham, and to his seed forever.

And it came to pass in those days, . . . that all the world should be taxed.

Joseph also went up from Galilee, out of the city of Nazareth, into Judea, unto the city of David, which is called Bethlehem, (because he was of the house and lineage of David,) to be taxed with Mary his espoused wife, being great with child.

And so it was, that, while they were there, the days were accomplished that she should be delivered. And she brought forth her first-born son, . . . and laid him in a manger; because there was no room for them in the inn.

And there were in the same country shepherds abiding in the field, keeping watch over their flock by night.

And, lo, the ANGEL of the Lord came upon them, and the glory of the Lord shone round about them; and they were sore afraid.

And the ANGEL said unto them, Fear not: for, behold, I bring you good tidings of great joy, which shall be to all people.

For unto you is born this day in the city of David a SAVIOUR, which is CHRIST the LORD.

And suddenly there was with the ANGEL a multitude of the heavenly host praising God, and saying, GLORY to GOD in the highest, and on earth PEACE, GOOD-will toward men.

And when eight days were accomplished for the circumcising of the child, his name was called JESUS, which was so named of the ANGEL.

And when the days of her purification according to the law of Moses were accomplished, they brought him to Jerusalem, to present him to the LORD.

And, behold, there was a man in Jerusalem, whose name was Simeon; and the same man was just and devout, waiting for the consolation of Israel: and the HOLY GUEST was upon him.

And it was revealed unto him by the HOLY GUEST, that he should not see death, before he had seen the LORD'S CHRIST. And he came by the SPIRIT into the temple: and when the parents brought in the child JESUS, to do for him after the custom of the law, then took he him up in his arms, and blessed God, and said, Lord, now lettest thou thy servant depart in PEACE, according to thy WORD: for mine eyes have seen THY salvation, which THOU hast prepared before the face of all people; a light to lighten the Gentiles, and the glory of thy people Israel.

And Simeon blessed them, and said unto Mary his mother, Behold, this CHILD is set for the fall and rising again of many in Israel; and for a sign which shall be spoken against; (yea, a sword shall pierce through thy own soul also;) that the thoughts of many hearts may be revealed.

And there was one Anna, a prophetess. . . . And she coming in that instant gave thanks likewise unto the Lord, and spake of him to all them that looked for redemption in Jerusalem.

And the child grew, and waxed strong in SPIRIT, filled with wisdom; and the grace of GOD was upon him.

Now his parents went to Jerusalem every year at the feast of the passover.

And when he was twelve years old, they went up to Jerusalem after the custom of the feast.

And when they had fulfilled the days, as they returned, the child JESUS tarried behind in Jerusalem; and Joseph and his mother knew not of it. . . . And when they found him not, they turned back again to Jerusalem, seeking him.

And it came to pass, that after three days they found him in the temple, sitting in the midst of the doctors, both hearing them, and asking them questions.

And when they saw him, they were amazed: and his mother said unto him, SON, why hast thou thus dealt with us?

And he said unto them, How is it that ye sought me? wist ye not that I must be about my FATHER'S business?

And Jesus increased in wisdom and stature, and in favor with God and man.

Now in the fifteenth year of the reign of Tiberius Cæsar, . . . the word of God came unto John the son of Zacharias. . . . And he came into all the country about Jordan, preaching the baptism of repentance for the remission of sins.

And as the people were in expectation, and all men mused in their hearts of John, whether he were the Christ, or not; John answered, saying unto them all, I indeed baptize you with water; but one mightier than I cometh, the latchet of whose shoes I am not worthy to unloose: he shall baptize you with the HOLY GUEST and with fire.

Now when all the people were baptized, it came to pass, that Jesus also being baptized, and praying, the heaven was opened, and the HOLY GUEST descended in a bodily shape like a dove upon him, and a voice came from heaven, which said, thou art my beloved SON; in thee I am well pleased.

And Jesus himself began to be about thirty years of age, being (as was supposed) the son of Joseph, . . . which was the son of David, . . . which was the son of Abraham, . . . which was the son of Noe, . . . which was the son of Adam, which was the son of God.

And Jesus being full of the HOLY GUEST returned from Jordan, and was led by the SPIRIT into the wilderness.

And Jesus returned in the power of the SPIRIT into Galilee. . . . And he taught in their synagogues, being glorified of all.

And he came to Nazareth, where he had been brought up: and, as his custom was, he went into the synagogue on the Sabbath day, and stood up for to read. And there was delivered unto him the book of the prophet Esaias. And when he had opened the book, he found the place where it was written, The SPIRIT of the LORD is upon me, because he hath anointed me to preach the gospel to the poor; he hath sent me to heal the broken-hearted, to preach deliverance to the captives, and recovering of sight to the blind, to set at liberty them that are bruised, to preach the acceptable year of the Lord.

And he closed the book, and he gave it again to the minister, and sat down. And the eyes of all them that were in the synagogue were fastened on him.

And he began to say unto them, This day is this SCRIPTURE fulfilled in your ears.

After that John was put in prison, Jesus came into Galilee, preaching the gospel of the KINGDOM of GOD, and saying, The time is fulfilled, and the KINGDOM of GOD is at hand: repent ye, and believe the gospel. —Mark 1. 14, 15.

And he said, I must preach the KINGDOM of GOD in other cities also; for therefore am I sent.

The Son of man came not to be ministered unto, but to minister, and to give his LIFE a ransom for many. —Mark 10. 45.

And Jesus answered and said, Verily I say unto you, There is no man that hath left house, or brethren, or sisters, or father, or mother, or wife, or children, or lands, for my sake, and the gospel's, but he shall receive a hundredfold now in this time, houses, and brethren, and sisters, and mothers, and children, and lands, with persecutions; and in the world to come ETERNAL LIFE. —Mark 10. 29, 30.

And Jesus said unto him, Let the dead bury their dead: but go thou and preach the KINGDOM of GOD, . . . No man having put his hand to the plow, and looking back, is fit for the KINGDOM of GOD. —Luke 9. 60-62.

And, behold, a certain lawyer stood up, and tempted him, saying, Master, what shall I do to inherit ETERNAL LIFE? He said unto him, What is written in the law? how readest thou? And he answering said, Thou shalt love the Lord thy God with all thy heart, and with all thy soul, and with all thy strength, and with all thy mind; and thy neighbor as thyself. And Jesus said unto him, Thou

hast answered right: this do, and thou shalt
LIVE. —Luke 10. 25-28.

Jesus said, Take no thought for your LIFE, what ye shall eat; ... The LIFE is more than meat. —Luke 12. 22, 23.

A man's LIFE consisteth not in the abundance of the things which he possesseth.
—Luke 12. 15.

Fear not, little flock; for it is your FATHER'S good pleasure to give you the KINGDOM. —Luke 12. 32.

And when Jesus was demanded of the Pharisees, when the KINGDOM of GOD should come, he answered them and said, The KINGDOM of GOD cometh not with observation: neither shall they say, Lo here! or, lo there! for, behold, the KINGDOM of GOD is within you.
—Luke 17. 20, 21.

Verily I say unto you, There is no man that hath left house, or parents, or brethren, or wife, or children, for the KINGDOM of GOD'S sake, who shall not receive manifold more in this present time, and in the world to come LIFE EVERLASTING. —Luke 18. 29, 30.

For he is not a God of the dead, but of the LIVING: for all LIVE unto him.—Luke 20. 38.

Then shall ye see the Son of man coming in a cloud with power and great glory. . . . When ye shall see these things come to pass, know ye that the KINGDOM of GOD is nigh at hand. —Luke 21. 27-31.

And when the hour was come, Jesus sat down, and his twelve apostles with him. And he said unto them, With desire I have desired to eat this passover with you before I suffer: for I say unto you, I will not any more eat thereof, until it be fulfilled in the KINGDOM of GOD. . . . For I say unto you, I will not drink of the fruit of the vine, until the KINGDOM of GOD shall come. —Luke 22. 14-18.

Ye are they which have continued with me in my temptations. And I appoint unto you a KINGDOM, as my Father hath appointed unto me; that ye may eat and drink at my table in my KINGDOM. —Luke 22. 28-30.

In him was LIFE; and the LIFE was the light of men. —John 1. 4.

Jesus answered, Verily, verily, I say unto thee, Except a man be born of water and of the Spirit, he cannot enter into the KINGDOM of GOD. —John 3. 5.

That whosoever believeth in him should not perish, but have ETERNAL LIFE. For God so loved the world, that he gave his only begotten Son, that whosoever believeth in him should not perish, but have EVERLASTING LIFE. —John 3. 15, 16.

He that believeth on the Son hath EVERLASTING LIFE. —John 3. 36.

Whosoever drinketh of the water that I shall give him shall never thirst; but the water that I shall give him shall be in him a well of water springing up into EVERLASTING LIFE.
—John 4. 14.

Lift up your eyes, and look on the fields; for they are white already to harvest. And he that reapeth receiveth wages, and gathereth fruit unto LIFE ETERNAL. —John 4. 35, 36.

Jesus said, He that heareth my word, and believeth on him that sent me, hath EVER-

LASTING LIFE, and shall not come into condemnation; but is passed from death unto LIFE. Verily, verily, I say unto you, The hour is coming, and now is, when the dead shall hear the voice of the Son of God: and they that hear shall LIVE. For as the Father hath LIFE in himself; so hath he given to the Son to have LIFE in himself.
—John 5. 24-26.

Marvel not at this: for the hour is coming, in the which all that are in the graves shall hear his voice, and shall come forth; they that have done good, unto the resurrection of LIFE.
—John 5. 28-29.

Search the Scriptures; for in them ye think ye have ETERNAL LIFE: and they are they which testify of me. —John 5. 39.

Labor not for the meat which perisheth, but for that meat which endureth unto EVERLASTING LIFE, which the Son of man shall give unto you: for him hath God the Father sealed. —John 6. 27.

Jesus said unto them, . . . The bread of God

is he which cometh down from HEAVEN, and giveth LIFE unto the world. . . . I AM the bread of LIFE. —John 6. 32-35.

And this is the will of him that sent me, that every one which seeth the Son, and believeth on him, may have EVERLASTING LIFE: and I will raise him up at the last day.
—John 6. 40.

Verily, verily, I say unto you, He that believeth on me hath EVERLASTING LIFE. I AM the bread of LIFE. —John 6. 47, 48.

I am the LIVING bread which came down from HEAVEN: if any man eat of this bread, he shall LIVE forever: and the bread that I will give is my flesh, which I will give for the LIFE of the world. . . . Jesus said unto them, Verily, verily, I say unto you, Except ye eat the flesh of the Son of man, and drink his blood, ye have no LIFE in you. Whoso eateth my flesh, and drinketh my blood, hath ETERNAL LIFE [partaketh of his twofold nature]. . . . As the LIVING FATHER hath sent me, and

I LIVE by the FATHER; so he that eateth me [partaketh], even he shall LIVE by me.
—John 6. 51-57.

It is the Spirit that quickeneth; the flesh profiteth nothing: the words that I speak unto you, they are SPIRIT, and they are LIFE. —John 6. 63.

Jesus said unto the twelve, Will ye also go away? Simon Peter answered him, Lord, to whom shall we go? thou hast the words of ETERNAL LIFE. —John 6. 67, 68.

Then spake Jesus again unto them, saying, I AM the light of the world: he that followeth me shall not walk in darkness, but shall have the LIGHT of LIFE. —John 8. 12.

As the Father knoweth me, even so know I the Father: and I lay down my LIFE for the sheep. . . . Therefore doth my Father love me, because I lay down my LIFE, that I might take it again. . . . And I give unto them ETERNAL LIFE; and they shall never perish. —John 10. 15-28.

Jesus said unto her [Martha], I am the RESURRECTION, and the LIFE: he that believeth in me, though he were dead, yet shall he LIVE: and whosoever LIVETH and believeth in me shall never die. —John 11. 25, 26.

And I know that his commandment is LIFE EVERLASTING. —John 12. 50.

Greater love hath no man than this, that a man lay down his LIFE for his friends.
—John 15. 13.

And this is LIFE ETERNAL, that they might know thee the only true God, and Jesus Christ, whom thou hast sent. —John 17. 3.

Jesus answered, My KINGDOM is not of this world: if my KINGDOM were of this world, then would my servants fight, that I should not be delivered to the Jews: but now is my KINGDOM not from hence.
—John 18. 36.

And many other signs truly did Jesus in the presence of his disciples, which are not written in this book: but these are written, that ye might believe that Jesus is the Christ, the Son of God; and that believing ye might have LIFE through HIS NAME. —John 20. 30, 31.

ACTS OF THE APOSTLES.

Unto the apostles whom he had chosen: to whom also he showed himself ALIVE after his passion by many infallible proofs, being seen of them forty days, and speaking of the things pertaining to the KINGDOM of GOD.

When they therefore were come together, they asked of him, saying, Lord, wilt thou at this time restore again the kingdom of Israel?

Thou hast made known to me the WAYS of LIFE; thou shalt make me full of joy with thy countenance.

And they laid hands on the apostles, and put them in the common prison. But the angel of the Lord by night opened the prison doors, and brought them forth, and said, Go, stand and speak in the temple to the people all the words of this LIFE.

In his humiliation his judgment was taken

away: and who shall declare his generation? for his LIFE is taken from the earth.
—Acts 8. 33.

And when they heard these things, they held their peace, and glorified God, saying, Then hath God also to the Gentiles granted repentance unto LIFE. —Acts 11. 18.

And when the Gentiles heard this, they were glad, and glorified the word of the Lord: and as many as were ordained to ETERNAL LIFE believed. —Acts 13. 48.

And when they had preached the gospel to that city, . . . confirming the souls of the disciples, and exhorting them to continue in the faith, and that they must through much tribulation enter into the KINGDOM of GOD.
—Acts 14. 21, 22.

God that made the world and all things therein, seeing that he is Lord of heaven and earth, dwelleth not in temples made with hands; neither is worshiped with men's hands, as though he needed any thing, seeing he giveth to all LIFE, and breath, and all things; . . . for in him we LIVE, and move, and have our being. —Acts 17. 24-28.

None of these things move me [Paul], neither count I my LIFE dear unto myself, so that I might finish my course with joy, and the ministry, which I have received of the Lord Jesus, to testify the gospel of the grace of God.
—Acts 20. 24.

And now I exhort you to be of good cheer: for there shall be no loss of any man's LIFE among you, but of the ship. For there stood by me this night the ANGEL of God, whose I am, and whom I serve, saying, Fear not, Paul.
—Acts 27. 22, 23.

PAUL TO THE ROMANS

For therein is the righteousness of God revealed from faith to faith; as it is written, the just shall LIVE by faith.

To them who by patient continuance in well-doing seek for glory and honor and IMMORTALITY, ETERNAL LIFE.

For if, when we were enemies, we were reconciled to God by the death of his Son: much more, being reconciled, we shall be saved by his LIFE. For if by one man's offense death reigned by one; much more they which receive abundance of grace and of the gift of righteousness shall reign in LIFE by one, JESUS CHRIST. Therefore, as by the offense of one judgment came upon all men to condemnation; even so by the righteousness of one the free gift came upon all men unto justification of LIFE. That as sin hath reigned unto death, even so might grace reign through righteousness unto ETERNAL LIFE by JESUS CHRIST our LORD. How shall we, that are dead to sin, LIVE any longer therein? Therefore we are buried with him by baptism into death: that like as Christ was raised from the dead by the glory of the FATHER, even so we also should walk in newness of LIFE. Now if we be dead with Christ, we believe that we shall also LIVE with him: for in that he died, he died unto sin once; but in that he LIVETH, he LIVETH unto God. Likewise reckon ye also yourselves to be dead indeed unto sin, but ALIVE unto God through Jesus Christ our Lord. . . . Yield yourselves unto God, as those that are ALIVE from the dead. For the wages of sin is death; but the gift of God is ETERNAL LIFE through Jesus Christ our Lord. For the law of the Spirit of LIFE in Christ Jesus hath made me free from the law of sin and death. For to be carnally minded is death; but to be spiritually minded is LIFE and peace. And if Christ be in you, the body is dead because of sin; but the Spirit is LIFE because of righteousness.

For I am persuaded that neither death, nor LIFE, nor angels, nor principalities, nor powers, nor things present, nor things to come, nor height, nor depth, nor any other creature, shall be able to separate us from the love of God, which is in Christ Jesus our Lord. If it be possible, as much as lieth in you, LIVE peaceably with all men. For whether we LIVE, we LIVE unto the Lord; or whether we die, we die unto the Lord: whether we LIVE therefore, or die, we are the Lord's.

PAUL TO THE CORINTHIANS.

If in this LIFE only we have hope in Christ, we are of all men most miserable.

For as in Adam all die, even so in Christ shall all be made ALIVE.

Forasmuch as ye are manifestly declared to be the epistle of Christ ministered by us, written not with ink, but with the Spirit of the LIVING GOD ... who also hath made us able ministers of the New Testament, not of the letter, but of the SPIRIT: for the letter killeth, but the SPIRIT giveth LIFE. For we that are in this tabernacle do groan, being burdened; not that we would be unclothed, but be clothed upon that mortality might be swallowed up of LIFE. Finally, brethren, farewell. Be perfect, be of good comfort, be of one mind, LIVE in peace: and the God of LOVE and peace shall be with you. Amen.

PAUL TO THE GALATIANS.

I am crucified with Christ: nevertheless I LIVE; yet not I, but Christ LIVETH in me: and the LIFE which I now LIVE in the flesh

I LIVE by the faith of the Son of God, who loved me, and gave himself for me. But that no man is justified by the law in the sight of God: for the just shall LIVE by faith. . . . He that soweth of the Spirit shall of the Spirit reap LIFE EVERLASTING.

PAUL TO THE PHILIPPIANS.

For me to LIVE is Christ, and to die is gain.

Holding forth the word of LIFE; that I may rejoice in the day of Christ, that I have not run in vain, neither labored in vain. . . . with other my fellow laborers, whose names are in the BOOK of LIFE.

PAUL TO THE COLOSSIANS.

Set your affection on things above, not on things on the earth. For ye are dead, and your life is hid with Christ in God. When Christ, who is our LIFE, shall appear, then shall ye also appear with him in glory.

PAUL TO TIMOTHY.

Fight the good fight of faith, lay hold on ETERNAL LIFE . . . Charge them that are rich in this world, that they be not high-minded, nor trust in uncertain riches, but in the LIVING GOD, who giveth us richly all things to enjoy; that they do good, that they be rich in good works, ready to distribute, willing to communicate ; laying up in store for themselves a good foundation against the time to come, that they may lay hold on ETERNAL LIFE.

Paul, an apostle of Jesus Christ by the will of God, according to the promise of LIFE which is in Christ Jesus.

But is now made manifest by the appearing of our Saviour Jesus Christ, who hath abolished death, and hath brought LIFE and IMMORTALITY to light in the Gospel.

And the Lord shall deliver me from every evil work, and will preserve me unto his HEAVENLY KINGDOM, to whom be glory for ever and ever. Amen.

PAUL TO TITUS.

In hope of ETERNAL LIFE which God that cannot lie promised before the world began.

Teaching us that, denying ungodliness and worldly lusts, we should LIVE soberly, righteously, and godly in this present world.

That being justified by his grace we should be made heirs, according to the hope of ETERNAL LIFE.

EPISTLE OF JOHN.

That which was from the beginning, which we have heard, which we have seen with our eyes, which we have looked upon, and our hands have handled of the WORD OF LIFE. For the LIFE was manifested, and we have seen it, and bear witness and show unto you that ETERNAL LIFE which was with the FATHER, and was manifested unto us.

And this is the promise that he hath promised us, even ETERNAL LIFE.

We know that we have passed from death unto LIFE because we love the brethren.

Hereby perceive we the love of God, because he laid down his LIFE for us.

And this is the record that God hath given to us ETERNAL LIFE, and this LIFE is in his Son. He that hath the Son hath LIFE.

These things have I written unto you that believe on the name of the Son of God ; that they may know that ye have ETERNAL LIFE, and that ye believe on the name of the Son of God. This is the true God and ETERNAL LIFE.

EPISTLE OF JUDE.

Keep yourselves in the love of God, looking for the mercy of our Lord Jesus Christ unto ETERNAL LIFE.

THE REVELATION OF JOHN.

To him that overcometh will I give to eat of the TREE of LIFE, which is in the midst of the paradise of God.

He that overcometh, the same shall be clothed in white raiment : and I will not blot out his name out of the BOOK of LIFE, but I will confess his name before my Father, and before his angels.

And after three days and a half the SPIRIT

of LIFE from God entered into them, and they stood upon their feet: and great fear fell upon them which saw them.

And he said, It is done; I am Alpha and Omega, the beginning and the end. I will give unto him that is athirst of the fountain of LIFE freely.

And another BOOK was opened, which is the BOOK of LIFE.

And the city lieth four square. . . . And there shall in no wise enter into it any thing that defileth, neither whatsoever worketh abomination, or maketh a lie: but they which are written in the LAMB'S BOOK of LIFE.

And he showed me a pure RIVER of LIFE, clear as crystal, proceeding out of the throne of God and of the Lamb. In the midst of the street of it, and on either side of the river, was there the TREE of LIFE which bear twelve manner of fruits, and yielded her fruit every month: and the leaves of the tree were for the healing of the nations.

Blessed are they who do his commandments,

that they may have right to the TREE of LIFE, and may enter in through the gates into the city. And whosoever will let him take of the WATER of LIFE freely.

Be thou faithful until death, and I will give thee a CROWN of LIFE. Amen and amen.

www.ingramcontent.com/pod-product-compliance
Lightning Source LLC
Chambersburg PA
CBHW032148160426
43197CB00008B/821